CONTENTS

Making The Leap	2
Build Your Team	47
Goals	65
Performance Management	88
Dealing With Challenges	99
Operational Excellence	112
About the Author	163

Thanks to Manu, Emily, and Fynn for always being there, Karan Jain for suggesting that I write this book, and all of the managers I've had in the past who have influenced me and contributed lessons learned that have made their way into these pages.

MAKING THE LEAP

Shifting from an individual contributor to a manager is pivotal in a software engineer's career. It's not just about moving from technical tasks and coding to team guidance but about a profound perspective and skill set shift. You're no longer just a technical specialist but a leader who orchestrates, empowers, and shapes the team's future.

I have observed that new managers often struggle in two areas when transitioning into their new roles. First, they tend to take some time to feel comfortable delegating tasks, especially when they used to be responsible for those tasks. Second, many new managers continue to be overly involved in a project's technical details, even though it is no longer their primary responsibility.

Your technical background is valuable, even if you're no longer the primary coder. It equips you with a deep understanding of your team's work, enabling you to provide guidance and make informed decisions. However, shifting your focus from producing code to helping your team thrive is crucial. Your role now includes mentoring, coaching, and removing obstacles to enable your team to deliver their best work. While your technical skills will guide your decisions, your ability to foster collaboration, manage resources, and inspire growth will define your leadership success. Embrace the challenge of nurturing a team, shaping its direction, and creating an environment that fosters innovation and success. You'll encounter more complexity and ambiguity than you did in your engineering role, but your technical background will serve as a strong foundation.

In the upcoming chapters, we will explore various aspects of engineering management, including leadership, goal setting, fostering a culture of excellence, navigating challenges, and embracing continuous learning. This book is designed to guide you through the exciting terrain of software engineering management, balancing technical expertise with the art of leadership.

Each chapter in this book can be read as a standalone handbook and is often written in bulleted format, so you can easily find the information you need. You will notice that some themes, such as clear and authentic communication, are repeated throughout the book. These foundational concepts will help you in many areas of your journey, and you can weigh their importance because these building blocks are present across a wide array of tasks you will face.

The Manager as a Mentor

You may think that once you move from IC to an engineering manager position, the team will work for you, and you will be wrong; now, more than ever, you will work for your team. You will need to balance the career development of your direct reports with project objectives and operational excellence - all of which can be daunting to a new manager. An effective way to accomplish both goals is to take on a mentor role with your team. A mentor takes on the role of a guide and advisor to help others achieve their goals. As a manager, you can be a positive role model, provide guidance, and share your expertise with your team members, or you can negatively influence the team. The choice is yours, and your path often dictates your long-term success. By taking on the mentor role, you can help your team members navigate challenges and achieve their full potential.

It's important to remember that your actions and words as a mentor and new manager can significantly impact your team members. As a mentor, you can inspire and empower your team members to reach their full potential. However, if you're not careful, your words and actions can also cause harm and hurt your team members. Therefore, you must be mindful of your approach and the impact that you're having on your mentees. By creating a safe and supportive environment, being open and honest, and offering constructive feedback, you can help your team members thrive and grow.

Leading a team effectively requires more than just delegating tasks; it demands a thoughtful approach to communication and personalized guidance. Leaders can create an environment where team members feel valued and empowered by fostering open communication, understanding individual strengths and weaknesses, and conducting regular check-ins. This enhances team cohesion and drives better performance and job satisfaction. Here are some strategies to effectively mentor your team members:

Foster Open Communication: When leading a team, fostering a culture where everyone feels heard and valued is essential. One way to do this is to follow the principle of "leaders speak last." As a leader, you should resist the urge to offer your opinion first and instead listen to what your team members say. Doing this creates space for everyone to contribute and ensures no one feels silenced or overlooked.

As a leader, your words and actions can powerfully influence your team members. Therefore, you should be careful not to impose your ideas or agenda on others. Instead, aim to guide and facilitate the conversation, allowing your team members to arrive at their conclusions. This will help them feel more invested in the process and improve outcomes.

Tailored Guidance: Understanding each individual's strengths, weaknesses, and interests is crucial to providing effective guidance. Take the time to get to know your team members personally, assess their skills, and identify areas for improvement so that you can adjust your leadership style based on both the individual and the task.

Situational leadership, introduced by Paul Hersey and Ken Blanchard in 1969, focuses on adapting leadership styles to suit the situation and the individual's development level. The model identifies four leadership styles: directing, coaching, supporting, and delegating, each suited to different readiness levels (R1-R4) based on competence and commitment. For instance, directing is for those new or lacking skills, coaching is for those with some experience needing guidance, supporting is for those with skills lacking confidence, and delegating is for those competent and motivated. Effective leaders adjust their style accordingly to facilitate growth and goal achievement. This approach underscores personalized leadership for optimal outcomes. For more information, refer to the Situational

Leadership website.

Regular Check-Ins: Regular one-on-one meetings with your direct reports and skip-level meetings can be incredibly valuable for you and your team members. These meetings offer leaders a dedicated time and space to provide feedback, offer guidance, and discuss progress toward goals.

One-on-one meetings allow leaders to understand better their team members' strengths, weaknesses, and work styles. This knowledge can then be used to assign tasks and responsibilities that align with each team member's unique abilities, ultimately leading to better performance and job satisfaction.

In addition, regular one-on-one meetings can help leaders identify potential issues or challenges early on before they become more significant problems. By addressing these issues proactively, leaders can help their team members overcome obstacles and stay on track toward achieving their goals.

You should reserve at least one one-on-one meeting monthly to discuss career development and progress. If you are a manager with skip-level reports, you should also set up one-on-one meetings with your skip-level at a cadence that may be quarterly.

As with almost everything discussed in this book, consistency is the key to success. Missing a scheduled one-on-one meeting with a direct report or skip-level report may be the easiest meeting for a manager to push out; however, you risk losing trust or sending a message that it's not a priority to your direct reports. The scheduled one-on-one should be kept, and at a minimum, if you realize you will need to reschedule, do so early and give the reason.

Knowledge Sharing: In addition to sharing your experiences, successes, and failures with your team members, there are several other effective ways to foster knowledge sharing within your team. For instance, you can organize lunch and learn sessions where team members can discuss a particular topic or idea. These sessions offer an excellent opportunity for team members to learn from one another and share their expertise.

Another effective way to encourage knowledge sharing is through demos. Team members can showcase their work to the rest, providing insights into their process, workflow, and decision-making. This can help team members better understand each other's work and learn from their approaches.

Team code reviews are also a great way to encourage knowledge sharing. By reviewing each other's code, team members can learn new techniques and best practices and identify areas for improvement. This can improve code quality and help ensure consistency across the team's work.

Fostering open communication, offering tailored guidance, and maintaining regular check-ins create an environment where team members feel valued and empowered. Utilizing situational leadership and encouraging knowledge sharing further enhances team cohesion and performance. Remember, your words and actions as a mentor have a lasting impact, so approach your role with mindfulness and consistency. By investing in your team's development and building a supportive culture, you achieve organizational goals and nurture a motivated, skilled, and cohesive team poised for long-term success.

Coaching vs. Managing

Coaching is about developing individuals by helping them enhance their skills and capabilities while managing, overseeing, and directing the team to achieve organizational goals.

Coaching

Coaching is another vital aspect of team development. While mentoring provides overarching guidance, coaching focuses on specific skills and performance improvement. Think of a sports team. The manager is like the head coach who sets the overall strategy, manages the team's resources, and oversees day-to-day operations. The coach is like an assistant coach who works more closely with individual players to improve their skills and performance.

The leader is like the team captain, who motivates and inspires team members, sets an example, and communicates the team's vision and goals. You will have to move between each of these roles as you guide your team.

Effective coaching involves identifying areas for enhancement, setting goals, and providing actionable feedback to help team members reach their potential.

Let's explore an example that illustrates the difference between coaching and managing in a software engineering context:

Managing

Consider a software engineering manager who oversees a team developing a new feature. In a managerial approach, the manager is likely to:

Assign tasks to each team member based on their skills, expertise, and preferences. Consider their previous experience, strengths, and areas for development to ensure a well-rounded distribution of responsibilities.

Monitor task progress regularly by scheduling check-ins and milestone reviews. Utilize project management tools and communication channels to stay updated on each task's status and address potential delays or roadblocks.

Offer solutions or direct guidance to team members who encounter problems by promoting open communication and a supportive team environment. Encourage team members to seek help and provide resources or mentorship to overcome challenges.

Conduct periodic performance reviews to evaluate whether team members have met their assigned tasks and achieved their goals. Use these reviews as an opportunity to recognize achievements, provide constructive feedback, and discuss potential areas for growth and development.

Now, consider a *coaching* approach in the same scenario:

Empowerment and Collaboration: The coach should collaborate with team members to understand their strengths, interests, and areas for development instead of assigning tasks. This involves empowering individuals to take ownership of their work.

Guiding and Asking Questions: Rather than monitoring progress closely, the coach should guide the team by asking questions that encourage critical thinking. For instance, "What challenges are you facing, and how do you plan to overcome them?"

Supporting Problem-Solving: When a team member encounters a problem, the coach should not provide immediate solutions but support the individual in finding their answers. This could involve asking questions like, "What options have you considered?"

Continuous Learning and Growth: Coaching emphasizes continuous learning and growth instead of periodic performance reviews. The coach provides regular feedback, focusing on outcomes and developing skills and capabilities.

In summary, while managing involves more direct control and task-oriented guidance, coaching fosters individual and team development by empowering individuals to think critically, solve problems independently, and continuously improve. Both approaches are valuable, and a skilled leader may integrate elements of both depending on the situation and the team's needs.

Effective coaching strategies are essential for fostering individual growth and aligning team efforts with organizational goals. One key strategy is setting clear goals by collaborating with team members to define performance objectives that match their aspirations and the company's needs. This alignment ensures that everyone understands their work, creating a unified direction. Additionally, providing specific and constructive feedback is crucial. Highlighting strengths and suggesting areas for improvement helps team members develop their skills and feel valued for their contributions.

Skill building is another vital component of effective coaching. Identifying skill gaps and offering opportunities for development through training, workshops, or hands-on experiences can help team members become more capable and well-rounded in their roles. Furthermore, recognizing and celebrating achievements, no matter how small, through positive reinforcement boosts morale and motivation, leading to enhanced performance and results.

While coaching focuses on immediate skill development and performance improvement, mentoring provides a broader scope for long-term career development and personal growth. A mentor shares experiences and advice, helping mentees navigate their professional landscape and build a strong network. This long-term relationship fosters deeper understanding and confidence, enabling individuals to reach higher leadership roles. Coaching and mentoring create a comprehensive support system that empowers team members to achieve their full potential and drive organizational success.

Create a Culture of Continuous Learning

As someone who has worked in software engineering for a while, I've realized that a willingness to learn continually can make or break a team. However, creating a culture that promotes active learning is challenging. It requires striking a balance between encouraging learning and maintaining productivity, and it can be difficult to motivate team members to take initiative in their learning. Despite these challenges, taking deliberate and thoughtful steps can cultivate an environment where continuous learning thrives.

As a leader, your behavior sets the tone for the entire team. This is what we call 'Role Model Learning '. Demonstrate your commitment to learning by actively engaging in professional development. Attend industry conferences, participate in workshops, and stay current with the latest trends and technologies. Share what you learn with your team through regular updates or informal discussions. Your enthusiasm for learning will inspire your team members to follow your example and prioritize their development.

Celebrate Failures that Push Technical Boundaries

Innovation often requires us to push the boundaries and take risks. This can lead to failures, but these failures are not setbacks. They are stepping stones on the path to success. Celebrating these failures creates a safe space for experimentation and learning. We encourage our team to view failures not as mistakes but as valuable learning experiences that contribute to our growth and innovation.

Ask Thought-Provoking and Open-Ended Questions

Encourage critical thinking and curiosity by asking thought-provoking, open-ended questions. These questions should challenge your team to think deeply about their work and explore new possibilities. For example, instead of asking, "Did you finish the task?" you might ask, "What challenges did you encounter, and how did you address them?" or "What alternative approaches could we consider for this problem?" This approach fosters a mindset of continuous improvement and discovery.

Connect Team Members with Different Viewpoints and Experience Levels

Learning is not a solitary journey but a collaborative one. Diverse perspectives can significantly enhance our learning and innovation. Let's intentionally connect team members with varying viewpoints and experience levels when assigning tasks. This cross-pollination of ideas can lead to fresh insights and innovative solutions. Let's encourage cross-functional collaboration and create opportunities for team members to learn from each other's expertise. This broadens our skill sets and strengthens our team's overall problem-solving capabilities.

Additional Strategies for Promoting Continuous Learning

To further promote continuous learning, consider implementing the following strategies:

Provide Learning Resources: Ensure your team has access to various learning materials, such as online courses, books, and industry publications. For instance, you could set up a shared drive where team members can upload and access relevant materials. Offer subscriptions to platforms like Udemy, Coursera, AWS Skillbuilder, and edX, and encourage team members to complete at least one course per quarter.

Support Attendance at Events: Encourage your team to attend conferences, hackathons, and tech meetups. These events can provide new insights and spark innovation.

Facilitate Knowledge Sharing: You create a safe and supportive knowledge-sharing environment as a leader. Use team meetings for this purpose, allowing members to present on topics they have recently learned about or projects they have worked on.

Encourage questions and discussions and ensure that everyone has a chance to contribute.

Offer Mentorship and Coaching: Pair less experienced team members with mentors who can guide their learning journey. Consider the mentor's expertise and the mentee's learning goals when pairing. Regular one-on-one coaching sessions can also provide personalized feedback and support, so schedule these sessions at least once a month and encourage open and honest communication.

Allocate Time for Learning: Dedicate specific time during the workweek for learning activities. This can help team members stay current without feeling overwhelmed by regular tasks. Emphasize the importance of this time and encourage team members to use it for self-study, attending webinars, or working on personal projects that contribute to their professional development.

By integrating these strategies into your team's daily routines, you can create a culture of continuous learning that drives innovation, enhances skills, and fosters a collaborative and dynamic work environment.

Who did you empower today?

Empowerment is the result of fostering personal growth and learning within a team. When team members feel trusted and capable, they are likelier to take ownership of their work, contribute ideas, and excel in their roles. Empowerment transforms individuals from mere contributors to valuable stakeholders who are deeply invested in their team's success. Here are some strategies to empower your team, each of which plays a crucial role in their personal growth and development:

Delegate Responsibilities: Assign tasks and projects that challenge your team members' skills and push them beyond their comfort zones. This will help them grow and build their confidence in handling more complex and critical tasks.

As a manager, your role is not just to assign tasks but to encourage ownership. Allow your team members to own their work fully. Provide guidance and support, but give them the autonomy to make decisions and learn from their outcomes. This fosters a sense of responsibility and accountability, leading to higher engagement and motivation.

Celebrate Autonomy: Recognize and appreciate instances where team members independently solve problems or make impactful decisions. Publicly celebrating these achievements reinforces the value of autonomy and encourages others to follow suit.

Recognize Contributions and Initiatives: Publicly acknowledge and appreciate your team members' efforts and initiatives. Regularly celebrating successes, both big and small, motivates individuals and reinforces a culture of recognition and appreciation.

Developing and empowering your team is not just a task; it's a crucial responsibility in successful software engineering management. As you lead your team members toward reaching their full potential, it's important to remember that your positive impact extends beyond just the projects at hand. You are shaping their career trajectories and cultivating a culture of growth. By fulfilling the roles of mentor, coach, and advocate for continuous learning, you elevate individuals and pave the way for collective success. Your influence is key in this process.

The Broader Impact of Empowerment

Empowering your team is not just about enhancing current performance but also about preparing for the future. When team members feel empowered, they are more likely to innovate, take initiative, and drive the team forward. This proactive mindset is essential for navigating the rapidly evolving landscape of software engineering.

Moreover, empowered team members are more likely to develop leadership skills, creating a ripple effect of growth and development within the organization. This strengthens your current team and builds a pipeline of capable leaders for the future.

Shaping a Culture of Growth

As a manager, your role goes beyond project management; you are instrumental in shaping the culture and future of your team. Promoting continuous learning, providing constructive feedback, and celebrating successes create an environment where team members are motivated to grow and excel. This culture of growth is a cornerstone of long-term success, fostering innovation, resilience, and high performance.

Team development isn't just about addressing immediate needs and laying the foundation for sustained success. It's about investing in your team members' growth and empowerment, ensuring they can meet future challenges and contribute to the organization's success. This long-term perspective instills a sense of hope and optimism, knowing that the efforts put into empowerment today will yield fruitful results in the future.

Communication and Collaboration

As you progress in your career, effective communication becomes increasingly important. As a manager, you must convey the broader vision of projects to the development team and translate technical jargon into understandable language for non-technical stakeholders. For instance, when discussing a new project with your team, you might say, 'Our goal is to develop a user-friendly app that meets our customers' needs.' this is because the scope of communication broadens as you move up the ladder.

As an individual contributor, you often focus on specific tasks and communicate with your immediate team. However, as a manager, you must communicate with diverse stakeholders, teams, and departments to ensure everyone is on the same page and working towards common goals. This requires a broader perspective and the ability to communicate effectively with people from different backgrounds and areas of expertise.

Your role as a manager is to act as a bridge between different departments and teams, linking them together and facilitating exchange and understanding. By orchestrating the code and acting as a central hub, you'll help connect the intricate project framework and ensure everyone is working towards the same objectives. To effectively bridge gaps, mastering the art of communication is not just crucial but empowering. Here are some techniques that you can consider to improve your communication skills:

Clear Messaging: Communicate your ideas, goals, and expectations concisely and in easily understandable language. Ensure that your message is well-structured and aligned with the recipients' needs.

Adaptive Language: Tailor your language to suit your audience. Use simple language when communicating with non-technical stakeholders, and dive into technical details when speaking to your development team.

Open Channels: Encourage available communication channels within your team and across departments. Encourage questions, feedback, and discussions to ensure a continuous flow of information.

Repetition: Say it once, say it often.

The Power of Active Listening

Effective communication involves not only speaking but also active listening, which is a skill that requires you to fully focus, understand, respond, and remember what is being said. Active listening can help you gain valuable insights, build stronger relationships, and make better decisions based on what you learn from others. To practice active listening, you should give your full attention, clarify what you've heard by asking questions, and try understanding the speaker's point of view.

When you take the time to listen carefully to your team members, they are more likely to feel comfortable sharing their thoughts, concerns, suggestions, and ideas. By considering their perspectives in your decision-making process, you play a pivotal role in creating a culture of collaboration and inclusivity that will benefit everyone.

For instance, let's say you're talking to a colleague who is expressing their concerns about a project. To actively listen, give them your full attention, make eye contact, and avoid interrupting them. You may ask questions to clarify any points you don't understand and rephrase what they've said to ensure you've understood correctly. This shows that you're not just engaged and interested but also that you respect their opinion and value their input.

When you practice active listening, it's essential to ask clarifying questions and avoid telling the speaker what you think they should do. Asking questions helps you understand the speaker's point of view and allows them to elaborate on their thoughts and ideas. It also shows that you're engaged and interested in what they say.

Furthermore, when you ask open-ended questions, you encourage the speaker to share more information and express themselves fully. Open-ended questions generally start with 'what,' 'how,' or 'why' and require more than a yes or no answer. For example, instead of saying, 'I think we should do it this way,' try asking, 'What do you think about doing it this way?' This approach allows the speaker to voice their opinion and allows both parties to contribute to the conversation, fostering a culture of collaboration and inclusivity.

On the other hand, when you tell someone what to do, you risk coming across as dismissive or controlling. It can also shut down the conversation and prevent the speaker from sharing their perspective. Instead, focus on asking questions that help you better understand the speaker's thoughts and feelings. Doing so creates a safe and respectful environment for open communication and collaboration.

Navigating Conflict and Resolution

Collaboration often leads to conflicts when differing viewpoints, priorities, and expectations clash. As a manager, you play a pivotal role in resolving these disputes. Conflicts should not be avoided but viewed as opportunities for growth and improvement, and your leadership is the key driver in this transformative process.

Transitioning from an individual contributor to an engineering management role brings new challenges, one of the most significant being the need for adept conflict resolution skills. Jeff Bezos, the visionary founder of Amazon, has shared valuable insights on navigating conflict, cautioning against the pitfalls of compromise as a "lose-lose" proposition. An effective leader must undergo a mindset shift and prioritize strategic decision-making that transcends conventional compromise.

Bezos challenges the traditional notion of compromise, suggesting that settling for middle-ground solutions may undermine the potential for innovation and excellence. Instead, you should approach conflict resolution with a commitment to finding novel solutions that benefit all parties involved. This approach aligns with the idea that authentic leadership involves creating a win-win scenario where conflicts are not merely resolved but transformed into opportunities for growth and continuous improvement.

Navigating conflict in an engineering management role requires empathy, communication, and decisiveness. Effective leaders strive to understand the underlying concerns of all stakeholders and facilitate open dialogue. This process allows for identifying shared goals and exploring alternative solutions that address the root causes of conflict.

Let's examine a practical example of conflict resolution in an engineering management role. Imagine two developers—let's call them Developer A and Developer B—disagreeing over the implementation of a feature. In this scenario, the manager can use the strategic leadership approach we've discussed to resolve the issue.

Instead of defaulting to compromise, the manager plays a crucial role in creating an environment where open and respectful communication is encouraged. Both developers should be allowed to express their viewpoints and highlight the rationale behind their proposed approaches. The manager guides the discussion beyond a simple compromise toward a more innovative and mutually beneficial resolution.

To achieve this, the manager can steer the conversation toward understanding the unique strengths and drawbacks of each developer's approach. Rather than settling for a middle ground that may dilute the feature's potential excellence, the manager can challenge the team to explore alternative solutions that address the core concerns of both developers.

For example, one approach could involve assigning leadership of the feature implementation to Developer A, leveraging their preferred method, while Developer B contributes support and feedback throughout the process. This strategic delegation not only allows for a more nuanced and specialized execution of the feature but also recognizes and values the unique technical expertise of each team member in conflict resolution.

By embracing conflict resolution strategies such as open dialogue, mediation, and empathy, the manager ensures that conflicts become catalysts for innovation rather than impediments to progress. Encouraging a mindset that goes beyond compromise and seeks win-win solutions, the manager resolves the immediate conflict and nurtures a culture of continuous improvement within the development team. Remember, conflicts are viewed not as obstacles but as opportunities for growth and collective success.

Building a Positive Culture

Remember, as a manager, your role is pivotal in shaping a team's culture, which significantly impacts productivity, performance, and the well-being of team members. You can cultivate a positive culture within your team by reflecting on your actions, values, and leadership style. This empowerment comes with a great responsibility but also opens up a world of possibilities for creating a thriving and fulfilling work environment.

Leading by example is the most effective way to create a positive team culture. You must be mindful of your behavior and ensure it aligns with the team's values and goals. You should also foster an environment where team members feel comfortable sharing their ideas and opinions and where you can have open and honest discussions. In addition, it is important to recognize and celebrate team members' achievements. This helps build morale and encourages team members to work hard towards their goals. By creating a culture that values hard work, collaboration, and open communication, you can create a team that is not only productive but also happy and fulfilled.

Setting the Tone: Your actions and decisions set the tone for this culture. For instance, if you prioritize open communication and encourage your team to share their ideas and feedback, your team culture will likely reflect transparency and collaboration. On the other hand, if you discourage dissenting opinions and micromanage your team, your culture may become more closed off and hierarchical.

Your communication style, approach to challenges, and interactions with team members contribute to the cultural environment you create. For example, suppose you are consistently respectful, empathetic, and fair in your dealings with your team. In that case, they are likely to feel valued and supported, which can encourage a positive and inclusive culture. Alternatively, suppose you are dismissive, critical, or display favoritism in your interactions with your team. In that case, they may become demotivated and disengaged from their work, leading to a toxic culture.

Always be mindful of how your actions impact your team's culture. Setting a positive tone and being intentional about your actions and communication can foster a healthy and productive culture that benefits your team and organization.

Build a diverse team.

An inclusive environment is where everyone feels welcomed, respected, valued, and supported, regardless of their differences. It is a space where people can express themselves freely and contribute to the team's goals without fear of discrimination, harassment, or biases. Inclusivity encourages diversity and promotes a sense of belonging, which leads to better collaboration, productivity, and overall job satisfaction. As a manager, you have the power to create an environment where all team members feel valued, respected, and heard, irrespective of their background, identity, or experiences. To create a culture of inclusivity, it is important to start with recruiting a diverse team of employees. This brings various perspectives, experiences, and ideas, leading to innovative solutions and a better understanding of user journeys. Once you have a diverse team, providing equal opportunities for growth, recognition, and advancement is important. This means ensuring everyone can access the same resources, training, and professional development opportunities. This will help ensure that no one feels excluded or left behind. Another important strategy for fostering inclusivity is to create channels for team members to provide feedback on inclusivity and take action on their suggestions. This could include regular team meetings to discuss diversity and inclusivity, anonymous feedback channels, or employee resource groups. By actively seeking out feedback and taking action on it, you can create a workplace culture that is inclusive and welcoming to all.

Overall, promoting inclusivity requires a concerted effort from everyone in the organization. By championing diversity, providing equal opportunities, and creating channels for feedback, you can create a workplace culture that is truly inclusive and supportive of all team members.

Supercharge Innovation

Innovation is vital for any organization to grow and evolve. It is the key to staying ahead of the competition and meeting customers' changing needs. However, innovation cannot thrive in an environment resistant to change and new ideas. As a manager, you create a culture that encourages experimentation, welcomes new ideas, and celebrates risk-taking. To foster innovation, you must create a safe space where employees feel comfortable sharing ideas and trying new things. This requires openness to new perspectives and a willingness to listen to your team's insights. You can encourage creativity by giving your employees the resources to experiment and explore unconventional solutions. Creating a culture of innovation also means embracing change. When you are open to change, you give your team the freedom to adapt to new situations and develop new ideas. By embracing change, you show your team that you trust them to make the right decisions and take calculated risks.

As a manager, you are not just a leader, you are a catalyst for innovation. By creating a culture that encourages experimentation, embraces change, and welcomes new ideas, you can help your organization stay ahead of the curve and achieve its full potential. Your role is pivotal in fostering innovation, and by embracing this role, you can inspire your team to think outside the box, take risks, and drive the organization forward.

Collaboration and Teamwork

Promoting collaboration and teamwork is crucial for success in software engineering projects. As a manager, your role is to foster an environment where collaboration is encouraged and ingrained in the team's DNA. Various approaches can achieve this.

One effective approach is to form teams that bring together diverse skill sets, promoting multidisciplinary collaboration. When team members come from different backgrounds and possess different expertise, they are more likely to approach problems from multiple perspectives, leading to more creative and effective solutions. This can be especially beneficial when tackling complex software engineering projects that require a wide range of skills.

Another approach is to align individual goals with collective objectives, promoting a sense of shared purpose. When team members understand how their contributions fit into the larger picture and how they ultimately contribute to the project's success, they are more likely to work together towards a common goal. Establishing clear project objectives and regularly communicating these to the team can achieve this.

Finally, providing tools and platforms that facilitate accessible communication, knowledge sharing, and collaboration can promote teamwork. By 'accessible communication, 'we mean easy-to-understand, readily available, and inclusive communication. This can include using collaboration software such as Slack or Trello and providing regular opportunities for team members to meet and share information. By providing these tools and opportunities, team members can easily communicate with one another, share knowledge and ideas, and work together more effectively.

Promoting collaboration and teamwork is crucial for success in software engineering projects. Managers can create an environment where teamwork is encouraged and fostered by using various approaches, such as forming diverse teams, aligning individual goals with collective objectives, and providing tools and platforms for communication and collaboration.

Conclusion:

When building a positive team culture, it's essential to remember that it requires intentional effort, dedication, and a commitment to values that foster inclusivity, innovation, and collaboration. As a manager, you significantly shape your team's environment and experience through your actions and leadership style. By embracing these values, you can create a positive work environment that impacts every aspect of your team's journey, leading to increased success and overall satisfaction.

Perfect is the enemy of good

The age-old adage, "Perfect is the enemy of good," is a timeless dilemma that professionals and teams face daily. Pursuing excellence often leads to two contrasting approaches: the relentless quest for perfection and the pragmatic acceptance of *'good enough.'* This section delves into the nuances of these approaches, exploring their benefits, pitfalls, and the art of discerning when to pursue perfection and when to embrace a more pragmatic mindset in your professional endeavors.

Striving for Perfection vs. Embracing "Good Enough":

Pursuing perfection is the relentless quest for the highest standard, eliminating errors, and creating flawless outcomes. It often involves meticulous attention to detail, exacting standards, and the desire to create something as close to perfect as possible. This can be viewed as a positive and negative trait depending on context. On the other hand, *'good enough'* is a concept that signifies accepting a level of quality or completion that meets the required standards but may not be perfect. It involves balancing time, resources, and the expected outcome. This approach acknowledges that perfection is often unattainable or not worth additional effort. Accepting 'good enough' allows quicker completion of tasks and projects, enabling teams to move forward and adapt to changing circumstances. It ensures that resources, such as time, are used effectively and not wasted on refining aspects that don't significantly impact the result. A *'good enough'* mindset can foster innovation and creativity, encouraging experimentation and risk-taking. By accepting that perfection is not always attainable or necessary, individuals and teams can experience a significant reduction in stress and a better work-life balance, providing a sense of relief and reassurance.

Potential Dangers of Perfectionism:

Perfectionism can have various negative effects, including diminished productivity, increased stress and burnout, missed deadlines, and underutilization of resources. Pursuing perfection can lead to overanalyzing and excessive revisions that waste time on minor details, slowing progress. This is especially true when perfectionism is applied to tasks that do not require such a level of scrutiny or functions that are not critical.

Perfectionism can create immense stress and pressure, which may result in burnout and negatively impact mental and physical health. Individuals who are overly concerned with achieving perfection may experience anxiety, frustration, and feelings of inadequacy. Excessive and prolonged stress can lead to burnout and emotional, physical, and mental exhaustion.

Focusing on perfection can cause delays and missed deadlines, which can be detrimental in a competitive or time-sensitive environment. This is particularly true when perfectionism is applied to tasks with clear deadlines or time constraints. Finally, perfectionism may lead to the overuse of resources, including time and money, without a commensurate increase in value or quality. This can waste resources that could be used more effectively elsewhere.

Benefits of Embracing *'Good Enough'*:

Embracing the concept of *'good enough'* can bring about several benefits. It allows for quicker completion of tasks and projects, enabling teams to move forward and adapt to changing circumstances. This is particularly true when the task doesn't require high precision or attention to detail. Resource Efficiency ensures that resources, such as time, are used effectively and not wasted refining aspects that don't significantly impact the result. This can be especially valuable when resources are limited, or the task is not critical. A *"good enough"* mindset can foster innovation and creativity, encouraging experimentation and risk-taking. Individuals not overly concerned with achieving perfection can focus more on exploring new ideas and approaches. By accepting that perfection is not always attainable or necessary, individuals and teams can experience reduced stress and better work-life balance. This can be especially valuable in high-pressure or competitive environments.

Trade-Offs for Making Progress

Making progress often involves making tough choices between different priorities. One of the most common trade-offs is between quality and speed. In some cases, it's crucial to balance these two factors to ensure that progress is made efficiently and with a high level of quality. However, taking a *'good enough'* approach to complete a task is sometimes possible, while perfectionism may be required in other situations.

Another important consideration when making progress is deciding how to allocate resources. While striving for perfection is desirable, it's important to consider the availability of resources and other essential tasks that may require attention. Therefore, it's essential to prioritize and allocate resources according to the task's importance.

Innovation often involves taking risks and exploring new ideas, which sometimes means moving away from perfectionism. Embracing a *'good enough'* approach can sometimes lead to significant innovation, but assessing the potential risks associated with a more relaxed approach is important.

Understanding stakeholders' and clients' expectations is crucial when deciding on trade-offs. Sometimes, perfectionism is necessary to meet their expectations, while a 'good enough' approach may suffice at other times. Effective communication with stakeholders is important; ensuring their expectations are met and progress is made accordingly is essential. This understanding fosters a sense of connection and responsibility, making the audience more aware of the impact of their decisions on others.

In summary, while striving for perfection is sometimes warranted, embracing *'good enough'* is also practical and essential for progress in many situations. Recognizing the dangers of perfectionism and being mindful of trade-offs can help individuals and teams make informed decisions that balance the pursuit of quality with the need for efficiency and innovation. Ultimately, the ability to discern when to aim for perfection and when to settle for 'good enough' is not just a skill; it's valuable in both personal and professional endeavors, empowering the audience with confidence in their decision-making abilities.

Thoughts on Tasking

As an engineering manager, prioritization and resource allocation are two crucial tasks that directly influence a project's success and the team's performance. Efficient resource allocation ensures that the available resources are well-balanced, maximizing efficiency and quality while maintaining high standards. Prioritization ensures the team works on the most impactful activities and critical tasks identified and aligned with business objectives.

By effectively allocating resources and prioritizing tasks, engineering managers can ensure timely, high-quality deliveries and feel empowered in their role. This process also enables managers to adapt to changing project needs and new priorities, making them better equipped to handle risks and challenges that may arise during the project.

Factors such as skill match, balanced workloads, and adaptability should be considered when allocating resources for a project. Assigning tasks based on team members' strengths and expertise can maximize efficiency and quality, while distributing tasks evenly can ensure that no one is overburdened. Preparing to reallocate resources as project needs evolve or new priorities emerge can also help ensure success. Software engineering often involves balancing competing priorities, which requires identifying critical tasks, aligning them with business objectives, and ensuring the team works on the most impactful activities. As a manager, your role in prioritizing your team is crucial and valued.

Dealing with competing priorities

Software engineering often involves balancing competing priorities. As a manager, you are responsible for prioritizing your team. Successful project management requires identifying critical tasks, aligning them with business objectives, and ensuring the team works on the most impactful activities. Here are some approaches to task prioritization:

Impact vs. Effort: Prioritize tasks based on their potential impact on the project's success relative to the effort required. This approach ensures that you focus on tasks that can significantly contribute to the project's success while efficiently using your time and resources.

However, it's crucial to remember that solely focusing on short-term wins without considering their long-term impact can have serious consequences. While short-term wins can bring immediate success and boost morale, they can also lead to a false sense of security and neglect of long-term strategies. Your team may be taking technical shortcuts to meet your requirements for fast delivery. Focusing only on short-term gains can lead to a lack of investment in long-term solutions, neglect of important tasks, and, ultimately, failure to achieve sustained success. As a manager, it's your responsibility to balance short-term gains and long-term strategies to ensure that you progress toward the project's long-term goals while celebrating short-term successes.

Therefore, when prioritizing tasks based on their potential impact and effort required, it's crucial to consider their long-term implications and ensure that you are not sacrificing long-term success for short-term gains. Remember, slow is smooth, and smooth is fast.

Urgency: When managing tasks and projects, distinguish between urgent and important tasks. Urgent tasks require immediate attention and have a deadline that is approaching quickly. On the other hand, important tasks are critical for a project's success but may not require immediate attention.

While addressing urgent tasks and prioritizing them accordingly is essential, it's equally important not to let them overshadow the critical tasks. Neglecting critical tasks simply because they don't have immediate deadlines can significantly impact the project's success in the long run, and it's an easy trap to fall into.

Urgent tasks can often be misleading and give a false sense of productivity as they demand immediate action, but completing them does not necessarily contribute to the project's success. It's essential to balance addressing urgent tasks and staying focused on the important ones to ensure the project's success is not compromised.

Therefore, allocating your time and resources wisely is crucial and ensuring you are not placing urgent tasks above important ones. Remember that important tasks may not have immediate consequences but can significantly impact the project's success.

Ensuring all tasks align with goals and objectives is important when managing a project. Each task should contribute directly to achieving the overall project goal and the broader organizational objectives. This alignment ensures that every task is meaningful and contributes to the project's success. It can increase efficiency, reduce waste, and improve project outcomes. To ensure alignment with goals, it's essential to review and assess the project plan regularly and to make adjustments as needed to ensure that all tasks are aligned with the project's goals and objectives.

As a manager, your role is crucial in successful software engineering projects. Execution is everything. It's not just about having a great plan or a brilliant idea. It's about putting that plan into action and making it a reality. You must clearly understand the project requirements, timelines, and milestones to execute your plan effectively. You must establish a resource allocation plan, including time, budget, and team members. Effective execution also requires a proactive problem-solving approach. You need to identify potential issues before they become significant roadblocks and take action to mitigate them. This proactive approach is key to ensuring the project stays on track.

In summary, execution is everything in software engineering projects. It's the difference between success and failure. By having a clear plan, allocating resources effectively, communicating with your team, and taking a proactive problem-solving approach, you can execute your plan successfully and deliver high-quality, timely projects.

Empower or Perish

Effective software engineering management requires a careful balance of delegation and trust. For instance, consider a scenario where you have a team member who is particularly skilled in debugging code. As a manager, it's important to thoughtfully delegate tasks related to debugging while considering your team's strengths and goals. You should communicate expectations, deadlines, and desired outcomes. Providing your team members with the necessary resources, information, and support is crucial for their success.

Trust is not just a nice-to-have in effective team management and successful delegation-it's the foundation. When you trust your team members to take responsibility for their tasks, you empower them and show them that you value their skills and contributions. This trust is built through transparency, consistency, and accountability, and it's a key factor in making your team feel valued and integral to the team's success. By trusting your team, you're not just delegating tasks but also delegating trust, which is a powerful motivator.

Finding the right balance between oversight and empowerment is key to achieving optimal results, which, in the context of delegation and trust, allows your team members to take on tasks and make decisions independently while still being accountable for their work. To this end, you should clearly define each team member's scope of responsibilities and decision-making authority, schedule regular check-ins to review progress and address concerns and trust your team members to make decisions within their areas of responsibility.

Delegation is not just about offloading tasks—it's about creating opportunities for growth and development. By delegating tasks, you're lightening your load and fostering an environment where your team members can develop new skills, enhance existing ones, boost their confidence and motivation, and prepare for higher-level responsibilities and leadership roles. This is a powerful way to inspire and motivate your team as they see their potential and value within the team.

In conclusion, delegation and trust are crucial skills in software engineering management. By delegating thoughtfully, building a foundation of trust, and striking the right balance between oversight and empowerment, you can create an environment where team members thrive, contribute fully, and achieve remarkable results. Remember that your ability to delegate with trust is a catalyst for creating a high-performing team.

The Challenge of Delegation for New Managers

Delegation, while vital for effective software engineering management, can be a daunting challenge for new managers. Transitioning from an individual contributor to a managerial role often involves a shift in responsibilities and mindset. New managers must navigate the delicate balance of delegation and trust, which can be tricky for several reasons. They may face challenges such as the fear of losing control, lack of experience in effective delegation, and a desire for perfection that can hinder their ability to trust their team members.

Fear of Losing Control: As an individual contributor, you were likely responsible for your work, ensuring its quality and timeliness. Now, as a manager, you must entrust tasks to your team members, which can be anxiety-inducing. There's a fear of losing control over the outcomes, which can be hard to overcome. One way to manage this fear is to start with small, less critical tasks and gradually increase the complexity and importance of the tasks you delegate. This can help you build confidence in your team's abilities and reduce your fear of losing control.

Lack of Experience: New managers may lack the experience and confidence to delegate effectively. They might be unsure how to assign tasks, whom to assign them, and how to communicate expectations.

Desire for Perfection: Many new managers come from technical roles where precision and attention to detail are paramount. They may have a natural tendency toward perfectionism, which leads them to believe they can complete tasks better and faster.

Concern About Team Performance: There's a natural concern about whether team members will perform to the same standard. New managers may question whether their team has the required skills and knowledge to handle tasks without constant oversight.

Uncertainty About the Team: If you're a new manager, you might still be getting to know your team members' strengths, weaknesses, and work preferences. This uncertainty can make delegation decisions more challenging.

Reluctance to Let Go: Transitioning to a managerial role may mean giving up tasks you've been comfortable with and enjoy doing. This can create reluctance to let go of responsibilities.

Time and Energy Investment: Delegation isn't a one-time task; it requires ongoing communication, guidance, and follow-up. New managers may be concerned about the time and energy required for effective delegation.

Like any new skill, effective delegation takes time to learn and master. As a new manager, you might feel the pressure to perform from day one and hesitate to delegate until you feel more confident. But remember, it's a learning curve, and with each task you delegate, you're one step closer to mastering it. So, be patient with yourself and trust the process.

As a new manager, delegation can be a challenging skill to develop. However, with time and practice, it can be mastered. One effective strategy for delegation is to identify your team's strengths and assign tasks accordingly. Another is to set clear expectations and provide support and resources for your team members to succeed. Finally, trusting your team's capabilities and allowing them to make decisions within their areas of responsibility is also a key strategy for effective delegation. Remember, delegation is not about giving up control but distributing tasks strategically to achieve better results collectively.

Remember that your role as a manager is to enable your team's success, which, in the context of delegation and trust, your team members can take on tasks and make decisions independently while still being accountable for their work. Delegation is a crucial tool to achieve that. Learning to delegate effectively can reduce your workload, empower your team members, promote their growth, and ultimately lead to higher team performance. By delegating effectively, you're not just offloading tasks but creating opportunities for your team members to learn, grow, and contribute to the overall success of your team.

In conclusion, although delegation can be a formidable challenge for new managers, it can be overcome by shifting mindsets, practicing effective delegation, and building trust. Mastering delegation is the key to success as a software engineering manager.

Self-Care and Growth

As a software engineering manager, your role in guiding and supporting your team is crucial. Equally important is the recognition that your mental and physical well-being is not a luxury but a necessity. Prioritizing self-care is not just about you; it's about enhancing your leadership skills, empowering you to navigate challenges, inspiring your team, and achieving lasting success.

Given the demanding nature of the job, managing your well-being can be challenging. Therefore, you must prioritize self-care to avoid burnout. Set boundaries to balance work and personal life, engage in stress-relieving activities like exercise, mindfulness, and hobbies, and ensure adequate rest and recovery time.

Recognizing the signs of burnout early is not just a management challenge but also an opportunity to take control of your well-being. As a manager, it's essential to identify these signs, such as constant fatigue, emotional detachment, and decreased productivity, and take immediate steps to address them. This proactive approach empowers you to prevent further negative impacts on your well-being and your team's productivity, fostering a healthier and more productive work environment.

Personal growth is not just a personal endeavor but a vital aspect of effective leadership that directly impacts your team's growth and success. Continuous learning, networking, and skill diversification benefit you and inspire and guide your team to learn and evolve. Enriching your leadership capabilities creates a positive ripple effect, fostering a culture of continuous growth and success within your team.

Balancing self-care and leadership responsibilities may seem daunting, but it is crucial for long-term success. Scheduling self-care activities, practicing reflection, and adjusting your routines to adapt to challenges are effective ways to achieve balance.

In conclusion, remember that self-care and personal growth are integral to your effectiveness as a leader in software engineering management. By nurturing yourself through self-care, avoiding burnout, and committing to continuous growth, you will set an example for your team and create a foundation of strength, resilience, and inspiration to influence you and your team positively.

Signs of Burnout

Recognizing the warning signs of burnout can help you take proactive steps to address it. For example, suppose you feel physically and mentally tired even after a full night's sleep. In that case, taking a step back and evaluating how to recharge and restore your energy is essential.

If you start to feel emotionally detached from your work or responsibilities, you can find ways to reconnect with your passions and purpose. Consider discussing your feelings with a trusted friend or colleague, and seek opportunities to take on new challenges or projects that reignite your enthusiasm.

If you notice a decline in productivity and efficiency, reassess your workload and priorities. Consider delegating tasks or seeking support from your team or supervisor.

Practice stress management techniques like mindfulness, meditation, or exercise to address increased irritability and frustration. It's also important to prioritize self-care activities that bring you joy and relaxation.

You should maintain physical health through proper nutrition, exercise, and rest to address physical symptoms. If necessary, seek medical attention.

Setting clear boundaries between work and personal life can prevent work-related stress from encroaching on your time. To avoid burnout, prioritize hobbies, exercise, and relaxation.

Remember to be kind to yourself and seek support from friends, family, or mental health professionals if needed. Addressing burnout can improve your well-being and give you renewed energy and enthusiasm for work and life.

Leading by Example

"You show loyalty, they learn loyalty. You show them it's about the work; it'll be about the work. You show them some other kind of game, and that's the game they'll play." - Daniels (The Wire)

In my experience in software engineering management, leading by example is essential to fostering a great team culture and driving success. It's a catchy phrase and a fundamental principle I try to live and breathe daily. As a manager, I see myself as more than just a leader—I strive to be a role model for my team, someone whose actions and attitudes can inspire and motivate others to do their best work.

The Ripple Effect of Leading by Example

It's important to remember that your behavior and actions as a manager significantly impact your team's culture and values. Setting a positive example can inspire your team to work together collaboratively and strive for excellence.

One key aspect of building a strong team culture is demonstrating dedication and a strong work ethic. When your team members see you are committed to quality and continuous improvement, they'll be more motivated to give their best.

Building trust with your team is another critical factor in fostering a positive work environment. Consistency between your words and actions is crucial, and transparency in communication can help create an environment where everyone feels comfortable speaking up and sharing their thoughts.

Of course, professionalism and ethics are also essential for successful software engineering management. As a manager, your adherence to ethical standards and professionalism will set the tone for the rest of your team. Demonstrating integrity, transparency, and accountability will create an environment where trust flourishes and ethical conduct is paramount.

One way to demonstrate your commitment to professionalism is through transparent communication. Keeping your team members informed about decisions and changes can help build trust and promote open dialogue.

Additionally, it's vital to prioritize ethical considerations when making choices that impact the team, projects, and stakeholders. By considering the ethical implications of your decisions, you can help ensure that your team operates with the highest standards of integrity.

Finally, it is essential to balance humility and confidence in your leadership style. Admitting mistakes, seeking input from team members, and showing a willingness to learn can help create an environment where growth and collaboration thrive.

In summary, leading by example is not just a responsibility but a privilege that empowers you to shape your team's culture and values. By embodying professionalism, dedication, and a strong work ethic, you set a trajectory for your team's success and growth and gain a sense of empowerment and confidence in your leadership journey.

As you journey through the chapters that delve into diverse dimensions of software engineering management, remember that your actions echo louder than words. By leading by example, you inspire greatness, foster collaboration, and create a legacy of leadership that resonates far beyond the present moment.

Personal Reflection and Development

As you reach the end of this chapter on software engineering management, turn the spotlight inward and reflect on your management style, strengths, and areas for growth. This self-awareness is not just a tool but a powerful motivator that inspires you to evolve, adapt, and thrive in the constantly changing landscape of software engineering management, fostering personal growth and development.

To begin your journey of growth, start with self-assessment. Critically evaluate your management approach, seeking insights into what's working well and needs refinement. Reflect on your interactions, decisions, and the impact you've had on your team. Honest self-assessment lays the foundation for targeted improvement.

Here are three questions to guide your self-reflection:

What are my management strengths, and how can I leverage them further?

Which areas of my management approach could benefit from refinement?

How effectively am I leading by example and embodying the qualities I expect from my team?

Continuous improvement is the bedrock of effective leadership. Armed with insights from your self-assessment, pinpoint areas where you can enhance your management skills. Whether it's refining communication, honing delegation, or fostering a more innovative environment, each step forward contributes to your growth as a manager.

To achieve your goals, set clear, achievable targets for improvement, focusing on one or two areas at a time. Encourage feedback from peers, mentors, and team members to gain insights from different perspectives. Regularly assess your progress toward improvement goals and adjust your approach as needed.

The journey of software engineering management is as much about personal growth as it is about guiding teams to success. To support your ongoing development, take advantage of available resources. Books, courses, workshops, and networking opportunities can all enhance your managerial skills.

In conclusion, the journey of software engineering management is perpetual, marked by growth, evolution, and the unwavering pursuit of excellence. By embracing personal reflection, setting growth-oriented goals, and engaging in professional development, you position yourself as a leader who guides others and embarks on a voyage of self-discovery and advancement. Keep this in mind as you delve into the subsequent chapters of this book, and remember that the path to excellence is paved with self-awareness, improvement, and continuous learning.

BUILD YOUR TEAM

When it comes to building a successful software engineering team, this chapter leaves no stone unturned. It covers the entire spectrum of team formation, from diverse expertise to the dynamics of effective teamwork. Moreover, it offers valuable insights on how to cultivate a work environment that not only encourages creativity and flexibility but also fosters a culture of excellence.

Tenets

Any team must have shared values and norms guiding its actions and interactions. These guiding principles define the team's identity and purpose and should align with its vision and mission. Established norms should outline acceptable behaviors and conduct. Aligning these guiding principles can create a cohesive and respectful atmosphere essential for effective collaboration and teamwork. When everyone in the team understands the tenets, they can work towards a common goal, knowing their actions align with the team's guiding principles. You may have noticed the inclusion of 'unless you know better ones' (UYKBO) at the end of tenets; this Amazon practice emphasizes change and a shared responsibility to keep striving to improve things. I strongly encourage you to empower your team to be the change they want to see wherever possible, fostering a sense of trust and responsibility.

Tenets are not just words on a page but fundamental principles or beliefs that guide and shape a group or an organization's behavior, decisions, and actions. In the context of an engineering organization, these tenets serve as a set of core values and norms that define the team's identity, purpose, and culture. They play a vital role in ensuring that every engineering team member shares a common vision and adheres to agreed-upon principles, directing your team's actions. For instance, the 'Security First' tenet is not just a slogan but a guiding principle that can lead your team to conduct regular security audits and address vulnerabilities promptly. The 'Precision in Execution' tenet is not just a phrase but a guiding principle that can lead your team to review code and design meticulously to ensure accuracy. Your team will use these to prioritize work and settle disputes.

I have created some sample principles that can guide your team if you run a tier 1 service with a strong emphasis on security and accuracy. These principles are not just suggestions but specifically tailored to address the unique challenges and requirements of our tier 1 service. They are designed to ensure that our work is always secure and accurate, and they are not just words but a roadmap for our team's success.

Security First: We prioritize the security of our systems and data above all else. Every team member plays a crucial role in identifying and addressing security vulnerabilities at every stage of development.

Precision in Execution: Accuracy in our code, design, and processes is paramount. We relentlessly pursue excellence in software development to ensure our tier 1 service meets the highest standards of accuracy.

Continuous Vigilance: We adopt a proactive approach to identifying and mitigating potential risks. Regular security audits and code reviews are integral to our development lifecycle to maintain vigilance.

Data Integrity Guardians: We view ourselves as stewards of data integrity. Building, maintaining, and validating data accuracy is a shared responsibility across the team.

Resilience as a Design Principle: Our systems are designed to resist challenges, including security threats and unexpected disruptions. We employ robust error-handling mechanisms and implement failover strategies to ensure uninterrupted service.

Ownership Mindset: Every team member takes ownership of the service's security and accuracy aspects. We encourage a culture of accountability in which individuals proactively address issues and continuously improve our systems.

Compliance Champions: We stay abreast of industry regulations and compliance standards relevant to our tier 1 service. Compliance is woven into our development processes, ensuring we adhere to the highest legal and ethical standards.

User Trust as a Core Metric: We recognize that user trust is earned through delivering secure and accurate services. Building and maintaining our users' trust is a key performance indicator for the success of our tier 1 service.

These tenets are a foundation for the team's culture and approach, guiding them to prioritize security and accuracy in every aspect of their work. Adapting and refining these tenets based on the team's evolving needs and the ever-changing software engineering and security landscape is essential.

Onboarding

Emphasizing the importance of onboarding new team members is crucial to ensuring they feel like a part of the team. A well-structured onboarding process, including mentorship, introduction to team workflows, and training, is essential to making them feel comfortable and integrated. This process sets the stage for seamless integration and accelerated contributions.

Establishing an effective onboarding process requires a few key steps. First and foremost, it's important to begin the process well before the new team member's arrival. This includes ensuring their workspace, equipment, and necessary software access are ready, planning their schedule, and introducing them to key team members. Assigning a mentor or buddy to guide them during the initial days is also crucial.

Once the new team member arrives, it's important to warmly welcome them and assign a mentor or buddy to guide them during the initial days. Clear expectations should be communicated, including the team's goals and objectives, the new member's role and responsibilities, and how their work aligns with the team's mission.

Providing access to relevant training resources and ensuring the new team member understands the tools, systems, and workflows the team uses are also essential. Encouraging mentorship or buddy systems can help answer questions and provide insights into team dynamics.

Regular check-ins should be scheduled to gauge the new team member's progress and address any challenges. Cultural integration should also be emphasized to ensure the new member understands the team's norms, practices, and expectations for respectful conduct.

New team members should be surveyed about their onboarding

experience, and this feedback should be actively used to adapt and improve the onboarding process for future team members. Encouraging participation in team-building activities and emphasizing the importance of ongoing learning and professional development can also help new team members feel valued and supported.

Celebrating milestones in the new team member's journey and publicly acknowledging their contributions can boost morale and encourage autonomy. Conducting a formal evaluation after a defined period is important to assess the new member's progress and integration into the team, and providing constructive feedback is essential.

Finally, it's important to remember that onboarding isn't limited to the initial weeks. Supporting new team members' integration over the long term and ensuring they remain engaged and aligned with the team's culture and goals is key to their ongoing success within the organization.

Structure and Organization

Team structure is vital in determining the success of a project. How a team is organized can affect how efficiently it develops software and collaborates to achieve its goals. There are different team structures, each with its benefits and challenges. Choosing the right team structure is crucial for delivering high-quality software products on time and within budget. I've added a few of the structures I have seen below for completeness. However, I prefer smaller teams with complete ownership and autonomy for a set of services to optimize speed, ownership, and the highest standards, as well as respect Brooks' Law.

Brooks' Law, articulated by Fred Brooks in his 1975 book The Mythical Man-Month, posits that adding additional personnel to a software project that is behind schedule will delay it further rather than accelerate its completion. This counterintuitive principle arises because new team members require training and integration, which diverts productive resources from the ongoing work. Furthermore, increased team size results in more complex communication and coordination challenges, exacerbating delays rather than alleviating them. Brooks' Law highlights the importance of managing software projects with careful consideration of team dynamics and the limitations of scaling human resources.

Functional software engineering teams consist of individuals with specialized skills in software development, such as front-end, back-end, database management, or quality assurance. While these teams excel in their areas of expertise, they may lack collaboration and focus only on their assigned tasks. This structure is suitable for projects that require a high level of specialized knowledge and skills.

Cross-functional software engineering teams consist of members with diverse technical expertise, such as developers, testers, designers, and product managers. These teams collaborate to build high-quality software products, which allows for a more holistic approach to problem-solving. However, effective leadership, clear communication, and a shared commitment to the project's success are crucial for the successful coordination of these teams.

Matrix teams combine aspects of both functional and cross-functional teams and are designed to be flexible and adaptable. These teams bring a balance of specialized knowledge and skills, with members having expertise in programming languages, web development, user experience design, quality assurance, and project management.

One advantage of a matrix team structure in software engineering is that it enables teams to pivot and adapt quickly to new technologies or changing requirements. By bringing together specialists in different areas, matrix teams can be more effective at problem-solving and develop more comprehensive solutions to complex challenges.

However, the matrix team structure in software engineering can also be complex in terms of decision-making and reporting. Members may report to multiple managers or leaders, which can create confusion or conflict if not managed effectively. Clear communication and well-defined roles and responsibilities ensure matrix teams function smoothly and effectively.

In recent years, the "two-pizza team" concept has gained popularity, especially in tech companies like Amazon. The idea is that teams should be small enough for two pizzas to feed everyone. This may seem minor, but it significantly affects team structure and dynamics.

The two-pizza team concept promotes smaller teams that can work more efficiently and collaboratively. With fewer people, communication is more streamlined, and decision-making is faster. This concept aligns with Brooks' Law of Communication, which suggests that adding more people to a late software project only makes it later due to increased communication overhead.

Smaller teams also foster a sense of ownership and accountability, as each team member significantly impacts the team's success. When teams are too large, individual contributions may get diluted, and accountability can diminish. Additionally, adding software engineering resources late in a project, especially to a large team, can lead to onboarding, knowledge transfer, and coordination challenges. This can further complicate communication and decision-making processes, ultimately affecting the project's timeline and quality.

Therefore, embracing the two-pizza team concept promotes efficiency and collaboration and aligns with principles that caution against overly large teams and late resource additions in software engineering projects.

Amazon's implementation of the two-pizza team concept also focuses on autonomy and decentralized decision-making. Each team is responsible for a specific project or area, and they are free to make decisions and prioritize tasks based on their understanding of the project's needs. This approach promotes innovation and creativity, as top-down directives do not constrain teams.

However, the two-pizza team concept is not without its challenges. Determining the right size for a team can be challenging and may require experimentation and adjustment. Smaller teams may also struggle with workload distribution and burnout, as fewer people share the workload.

Another critical aspect of effective software engineering management that aligns with the two-pizza-team approach is ensuring the team is responsible for the operational load. This means that the team is accountable for delivering features and the smooth operation of the software in production. When the team takes ownership of the operational load, it ensures accountability regardless of the team composition. It also promotes a culture of collaboration and shared responsibility, where team members work together to resolve issues and improve processes. Effective management involves creating an environment where the team feels empowered to take ownership of their work and are supported in their efforts to deliver high-quality software.

Make decisions on paper

Embrace a writing culture, a powerful tool that ensures thorough analysis and deep understanding of problems and alternatives. This culture compels individuals to think critically, articulate their thoughts clearly, and consider all facets of an issue. It's a meticulous approach that has been proven to be effective, as demonstrated by leading companies like Amazon, where a writing culture is deeply ingrained in their decision-making processes.

Amazon's commitment to concise and effective decision-making is evident in its use of one-page decision documents (OPDs). These OPDs are not just documents; they're a streamlined method designed to capture key information and the rationale behind significant decisions, all in a single-page format. The process typically involves a structured template that includes sections for context, alternatives considered, decision rationale, risks, and action items. This format ensures decision-makers have all the necessary information at a glance, facilitating quick but informed choices.

The importance of clarity, brevity, and data-driven reasoning is not just a part of Amazon's OPDs; it's a cornerstone of their decision-making process. These documents often undergo rigorous review and approval processes involving relevant stakeholders, ensuring transparency and alignment before implementation. This method isn't just about writing; it promotes transparency and alignment in decision-making. It helps Amazon's software engineering teams make timely decisions, maintains transparency, and drives efficient execution of projects, highlighting the crucial role of writing in promoting these aspects in decision-making.

Other companies also benefit from a writing culture. For example, Google uses design documents extensively to outline new project ideas, providing a clear vision and plan before development begins. Similarly, Netflix relies on extensive written documentation to ensure alignment and clarity across its distributed teams, promoting a culture of thoughtful and informed decision-making.

By embracing a writing culture, organizations can empower their employees to foster an environment where thoughtful analysis, clarity, and efficient decision-making are the norms. Writing forces individuals to delve deep into details, consider multiple perspectives, and articulate their reasoning clearly. This leads to more robust and well-considered decisions, demonstrating the value and impact of a writing culture in the decision-making process.

How to Embrace a Writing Culture in Practice

Set Clear Expectations and Provide Training: Start by setting clear expectations about the role of writing within your organization. Communicate the benefits of a writing culture and provide training on effective writing techniques. Offer workshops or seminars on structuring documents, writing concisely, and using data to support arguments. Encourage employees to see writing as a task and a vital part of the decision-making process.

Implement Structured Templates: Develop and implement templates for various documents, such as decision memos, project proposals, and meeting notes. These templates should include sections for context, objectives, alternatives considered, decision rationale, risks, and next steps. Standardizing the format makes it easier for writers to focus on content and for readers to grasp the key points quickly. For example, Amazon's one-page decision documents (OPDs) serve as a model, ensuring that all critical information is presented concisely and systematically.

Encourage Iterative Review and Feedback: Establish a process for iterative review and feedback. This collaborative approach ensures that multiple perspectives are considered and potential issues are identified early, making everyone feel included in the decision-making process. Create a culture where feedback is constructive and aimed at improving the document's quality. At Amazon, for instance, OPDs often undergo rigorous review and approval processes to ensure alignment and consensus.

Integrate Writing into Meetings and Decision-Making: Incorporate written documents into meetings and decision-making processes. Start meetings with a few minutes of silent reading of the relevant documents, allowing participants to understand the context and details before discussions begin fully. This practice ensures that everyone is on the same page and that discussions are more focused and productive. Encourage leaders to model this behavior by consistently using written documents to support their decisions.

Use Writing for Accountability and Transparency: Leverage writing to enhance accountability and transparency within the organization. Require written documentation for significant decisions, project milestones, and post-mortem analyses. These documents should be accessible to all relevant stakeholders and provide a clear record of what was decided, why, and expected outcomes. This practice keeps everyone informed and serves as a valuable reference for future decisions and learning.

Foster a Culture of Continuous Improvement: Promote a culture of continuous improvement by regularly reviewing and refining your writing practices. Solicit employee feedback on the effectiveness of current templates and processes and be open to making adjustments. Encourage sharing of best practices and lessons learned across teams. Recognize and reward individuals who excel in producing high-quality written documents, reinforcing the importance of writing within your organization.

By systematically integrating these practices, you can cultivate a writing culture that enhances critical thinking, ensures thorough analysis, and leads to better decision-making. This approach improves individual and team performance and drives overall organizational success.

Recognition and Motivation

Recognizing and motivating team members is crucial to inspiring them to perform at their best. Celebrating big and small achievements boosts morale and fosters a sense of accomplishment. Instead of relying solely on monetary rewards, it is crucial to provide growth opportunities, meaningful projects, and a supportive work environment that aligns with each team member's aspirations.

Three effective strategies for recognizing and motivating team members can help improve employee engagement and job satisfaction: meaningful work, growth opportunities, and regular feedback.

First, meaningful work is not just a task; it's an essential factor in employee motivation. Assigning tasks aligned with team member's strengths and interests helps them feel more connected to their work and the organization's mission, increasing their sense of purpose and job satisfaction. Your role as managers and leaders becomes crucial in aligning these two.

Secondly, growth opportunities are critical in keeping employees motivated and engaged. Offering paths for career progression and skill enhancement can give team members a sense of direction in their careers and a clear understanding of how to develop their skills. This can lead to better job performance, increased confidence, and higher job satisfaction.

Lastly, providing regular feedback is not just a formality; it's crucial for guiding improvement and growth. Your feedback helps team members understand how they are doing and what they must focus on to improve. This can be done through regular performance reviews, one-on-one meetings, or ongoing feedback sessions. Your constructive feedback can help team members feel supported and valued, leading to better performance and job satisfaction.

Implementing these three strategies can help organizations create a motivated and engaged workforce. Organizations can improve employee engagement and job satisfaction by providing meaningful work, growth opportunities, and regular feedback, ultimately driving better business results.

Adapting to Change

As software engineering evolves, change is a fundamental aspect that requires continuous adaptation. Teams must respond flexibly to technological changes, market demands, and project priorities. Fostering innovation and resilience is essential to enable team members to experiment, learn from their failures, and embrace change. Being agile when navigating change ensures the team can work harmoniously together and achieve success.

Below are some strategies that can help teams adapt to change:

Embrace an Agile Mindset: Adopt agile methodologies to enhance flexibility and responsiveness.

Encourage Continuous Improvement: By fostering an environment that values and encourages process improvements and innovative ideas, teams can feel motivated and inspired to contribute to the ongoing success of the project.

Learn from Setbacks: By analyzing failures and extracting valuable lessons, teams can feel reassured and confident in their ability to overcome challenges and avoid recurrence.

Amazon has a unique approach to learning from mistakes and correcting errors. The company's founder and CEO, Jeff Bezos, has emphasized the importance of embracing failure and using it as an opportunity to learn and grow. Amazon's approach to mistakes is encapsulated in its motto: "Fail fast, fail often."

One way Amazon learns from mistakes is through its 'post-mortem' process. After a mistake or failure occurs, the team responsible for the project conducts a post-mortem analysis. This analysis involves a thorough and honest examination of the event, including identifying what went wrong, why it went wrong, and how to prevent it from happening again. The analysis is conducted by everyone involved in the project, from the team members to the executives, ensuring a comprehensive understanding of the failure.

Another way Amazon learns from mistakes is through its 'two-pizza team' approach. This approach involves creating small teams of at most ten people who work on a project together. The concept behind this approach is that a team should be small enough to be fed with two pizzas, which encourages effective communication and faster decision-making. This approach also allows the team to take ownership of the project and be more accountable, leading to a higher commitment and dedication.

Amazon also encourages innovation and experimentation in its culture. Its 'Day One' program is designed to encourage employees to think like entrepreneurs and develop and test new ideas, even if they fail. This program is based on the idea that every day should be approached with the same level of enthusiasm and innovation as the first day of a startup. By fostering this mindset, Amazon stays ahead of the curve and continuously improves its products and services.

Amazon's approach to learning from mistakes and correcting errors is unique and effective. By embracing failure, conducting post-mortem analyses, creating small teams, and encouraging innovation and experimentation, Amazon has become a leader in the tech industry and continues to push the boundaries of what is possible. With these strategies, you can become the leader who shapes a successful team. Start implementing these strategies today and see the positive impact on your team's ability to adapt to change and foster innovation.

GOALS

As a software engineering manager, it is essential to define the purpose and goals of your team. This will act as a compass to guide your journey and chart a course that aligns your team's efforts with the organization's vision. Clear and well-defined goals are the heart of every high-performing software engineering team. They not only provide a roadmap for achievement but also infuse a strong sense of purpose into your team, shaping its identity and fostering a sense of belonging. In this chapter, we will explore the importance of goal-setting and purpose-definition. We will examine how these elements optimize resource allocation, ensuring that resources are channeled effectively. In the subsequent section, we will delve into the crucial significance of establishing clear goals.

Goal Setting and Alignment

As a manager, your role is not just important; it's pivotal. You are the key to ensuring the successful execution of your organization's vision and strategic objectives. Your primary responsibility is to bridge the gap between company-wide aspirations and the actual implementation of those ideas. This requires you to act as a conduit through which the organization's overall goals flow into actionable roadmaps for your team. Your contribution is not just valuable, it's indispensable in this process.

As a manager, one of your most empowering skills is the ability to simplify complex objectives into practical tasks. This involves breaking down the overarching vision into smaller, more manageable steps your team can execute. By doing so, you can help your team better understand the big picture and how their work contributes to the organization's overall success.

Ultimately, your ability to translate the organization's vision into practical tasks is essential for achieving strategic success. As a manager, you are responsible for ensuring that your team understands the organization's goals and clearly understands how their work contributes to the company's overall success. Doing so can help your team stay motivated and focused on achieving the company's objectives.

Aligning Team Goals with Company Objectives

Setting goals isn't just about making a to-do list; it's about ensuring those tasks fit the bigger picture. When a team's goals align with individual dreams and company-wide targets, it creates a powerful synergy. Team members realize how their work impacts the organization's vision, which not only boosts their motivation but also enhances their engagement. So, aligning goals is not just a plan but a key to success as a team.

Clarity of Purpose means communicating the company's

mission, vision, and objectives to your team. This helps your team understand the 'why' behind their tasks and motivates them to work towards achieving the common goal. But it's equally important to involve your team members in goal-setting. This not only ensures the goals resonate with their skills and aspirations, but also creates a sense of ownership. So, don't just set goals for your team; involve them in the process and see the difference it makes.

For example, a software engineering company in the project management software business aims to develop software enabling teams to work more efficiently and effectively, leading to increased productivity and better client outcomes. They aim to develop cutting-edge project management software that streamlines project workflows, enhances collaboration, and improves productivity by 30% within 12 months. They plan to involve their software engineering team in goal-setting to align their goals with the company's objectives and create a sense of ownership among team members.

This chapter will explore various goal-setting frameworks and strategies to enhance team performance and alignment. We will delve into the principles of SMART Goals, the structure of OKRs, and the importance of Collaborative Goal Setting. Additionally, we will discuss how to balance short-term goals with long-term objectives to ensure sustained success. Finally, we will cover methods for measuring progress and ensuring accountability.

Get SMART

In the dynamic landscape of software development, setting clear, actionable goals is crucial for guiding your team's efforts and ensuring project success. SMART goals fine-tune your team's focus, transforming ambitious intentions into achievable strategies. The SMART framework—Specific, Measurable, Achievable, Relevant, and Time-bound—provides a comprehensive approach to goal-setting that can drive your team toward excellence. In this chapter, we will delve into each component of the SMART acronym, exploring how it empowers you to set realistic and inspiring goals that lead to tangible results.

Specific: Clarity Leads to Action

A specific goal is precise and clear, leaving no room for ambiguity or misinterpretation. This precision is essential in ensuring that all team members understand the objective and their role in achieving it. Instead of a vague objective like "improve user experience," a specific goal would be "reduce app loading time by 20% to enhance user experience." This clarity lets your team focus on a concrete target, understand the expected outcome, and identify the necessary steps.

Example in Practice: Consider a project aiming to improve a mobile application's performance. A specific goal would be: "Optimize the app's code to decrease loading times from 5 seconds to 4 seconds within the next quarter." This specific target provides a clear direction and tangible outcome to work towards, making planning and executing the necessary actions easier.

Measurable: Tracking Progress and Success

Measurable goals provide criteria for tracking progress and determining success. They answer questions like "How much?" or "How many?" ensuring that your objectives are quantifiable.

This measurability allows you to monitor advancements, make data-driven decisions, and celebrate milestones.

Example in Practice: If your goal is to enhance customer satisfaction, a measurable objective might be "Increase the customer satisfaction rating by 15 points on the annual survey." This goal provides a clear metric for success and helps adjust strategies if the target is unmet.

Achievable: Balancing Ambition and Realism

While ambition drives innovation, goals must be attainable within your team's capabilities and resources. Setting unattainable goals can lead to frustration and burnout, undermining morale and productivity. Achievable goals should stretch your team's potential without breaking it, encouraging growth and continuous improvement.

Example in Practice: For a development team, an achievable goal might be: "Complete the integration of the new payment gateway within the next two sprints." Considering the team's current workload and expertise, this goal is challenging yet feasible.

Relevant: Aligning with Mission and Strategy

A relevant goal aligns with your team's mission and contributes directly to the organization's objectives. It should resonate with your team's purpose and the broader strategy, ensuring that efforts are directed towards meaningful and impactful outcomes.

Example in Practice: If your organization's strategic objective is to expand into new markets, a relevant goal for your team could be: "Localize the app for three new regions within the next six months." This goal supports the overall strategy and gives your team a clear sense of contribution to the company's growth.

Time-bound: Creating Urgency and Accountability

Setting a well-defined timeframe for achieving the goal infuses urgency and accountability into the process. A time-bound goal creates a sense of purpose and a clear focus point, helping the team prioritize tasks and manage time effectively.

Example in Practice: A time-bound goal for a team working on a new feature could be: "Release the new user dashboard by the end of Q3." This deadline ensures the team remains focused and driven to meet the target within the specified period.

Implementing SMART Goals: A Step-by-Step Guide

1. Identify Objectives: Understand your organization's overarching objectives and how your team can contribute.

2. Define Specific Goals: Translate these objectives into specific, actionable goals. Ensure each goal is unambiguous.

3. Ensure Measurability: Determine how you will measure progress and success. Establish key performance indicators (KPIs) that align with your goals.

4. Evaluate Achievability: Assess the feasibility of each goal, considering your team's capabilities, resources, and constraints. Adjust as necessary to maintain balance.

5. Check Relevance: Align your goals with the team's mission and the broader organizational strategy. Ensure that each goal contributes meaningfully to these larger aims.

6. Set Timeframes: Assign realistic deadlines to each goal. Break down the timeline into manageable milestones to keep the team on track.

Mastering the SMART goal framework is essential for any team aiming to achieve excellence in software engineering. Setting Specific, Measurable, Achievable, Relevant, and Time-bound goals provides your team with a clear roadmap to success. This structured approach enhances focus and productivity and fosters a sense of purpose and accomplishment. As you lead your team through the intricacies of software development, remember that SMART goals are more than just a planning tool—they are a catalyst for innovation, growth, and sustained success.

OKRs

OKRs, which stand for Objectives and Key Results, are a strategic framework that helps connect the company's high-level objectives with actionable results. An OKR consists of an Objective, which describes the desired outcome, and Key Results, which are measurable and trackable results that help measure progress toward achieving the objective.

OKRs empower the team by allowing them to focus on specific, trackable goals. This strategic framework provides a bridge between aspiration and accomplishment, making it easier for the team to align their efforts with the overarching company strategy.

Example OKR:

Objective: Improve Product Reliability

Key Results:

> 1. Reduce system downtime by 20% in the next quarter.
>
> 2. Achieve a customer-reported bug rate of less than 1%.
>
> 3. Conduct a comprehensive code review to identify and address performance bottlenecks.

The effectiveness of OKRs lies in their alignment. Objectives cascade down from high-level company goals, guiding your team's focus. Key Results provide measurable markers that track progress and success, giving you confidence in the OKR framework.

Connecting SMART Goals and OKRs

SMART goals and OKRs are not isolated concepts; they synergize to create a powerful orchestra of achievement. This collaborative approach provides the structure and specificity necessary to craft impactful OKRs. When you set an Objective using the OKR framework, the SMART criteria guide the definition of Key Results that are quantifiable, achievable, and time-bound.

Imagine your team's OKR is to "Enhance Security Measures." Applying the SMART framework, you might define Key Results such as "Conduct a security audit to identify and address vulnerabilities in the next two months," ensuring that the OKR is Specific, Measurable, Achievable, Relevant, and Time-bound.

Conclusion

In software engineering management, SMART goals and OKRs work together to help your team perform better. By setting Specific, Measurable, Achievable, Relevant, and Time-bound goals, you can ensure that your team's efforts align with the organization's broader objectives. The OKR framework links these goals with the bigger picture, fostering a culture of purpose, progress, and strategic alignment.

As you progress, remember the importance of using SMART goals and OKRs to guide your team toward success. With the right approach, you can create a plan that benefits everyone involved and helps your team achieve its goals. Now, it's time to take action. Start implementing OKRs and SMART goals in your software engineering management practices and see the positive impact on your team's performance.

Collaborative Goal-Setting

Effective software engineering management thrives on a collaborative approach, where team members are not just participants but key contributors in setting and working towards achieving goals. Collaborative goal-setting is a platform that values the insights of team members with diverse backgrounds and expertise, empowering them to shape the direction of the project. When team members are actively involved in the goal-setting process, their unique perspectives are not only acknowledged but celebrated, helping to uncover blind spots and identify areas for improvement.

Collaborative goal-setting brings a host of benefits, one of the most rewarding being the sense of ownership and accountability it instills in team members. When team members are not just part of the process but the driving force behind it, they feel a deep pride in their work and the outcomes it produces. This pride can be a powerful motivator, significantly increasing productivity and job satisfaction.

Another exciting benefit of collaborative goal-setting is its potential to foster a sense of camaraderie and inspire creative thinking and innovation. Brainstorming sessions and workshops are not just opportunities to share ideas, but platforms for team members to inspire each other and build on each other's insights. This collaborative environment can lead to developing new and innovative approaches, which can be the key to achieving breakthroughs and staying ahead of the competition, fostering a sense of connection and innovation in the team.

Overall, collaborative goal-setting is a powerful tool that can help teams to achieve great things. However, it's important to note that managing diverse perspectives and ensuring everyone's voice is heard can also be challenging. Similarly, quantitative and qualitative metrics can be complex, requiring balancing objective data with subjective insights. Despite these challenges, when team members come together to work towards a common goal, they can achieve amazing results that would be impossible to achieve on their own. By leveraging team members' diverse perspectives, skills, and expertise, organizations can drive innovation, increase productivity, and achieve success in all areas of software engineering management.

Quantitative and Qualitative Metrics

When achieving goals, it's essential to use both quantitative and qualitative metrics to measure success. Quantitative metrics provide measurable data, such as project completion time and defect rate, while qualitative metrics provide insight into user satisfaction, code maintainability, and overall user experience.

For instance, let's consider a software development team tasked with building a new mobile application. The number of downloads, user retention rate, and average session duration are quantitative metrics that can measure the project's success. These metrics provide factual data that can be easily measured and compared. On the other hand, qualitative metrics could be obtained through user surveys and reviews, which can provide insight into user satisfaction, ease of use, and overall experience with the app. While not as easily quantifiable, these metrics offer valuable insights into the user's perspective. By combining these quantitative and qualitative metrics, the development team can better understand the app's success and areas for improvement. This could involve optimizing the user interface based on user feedback or adding new features that users request, as the qualitative metrics indicate.

Considering both quantitative and qualitative metrics for a comprehensive project or product performance assessment is crucial. Quantitative metrics provide factual data, while qualitative metrics offer insights into user perspectives. This creates a balanced view of goal achievement, accounting for performance and experience. Addressing both aspects drives holistic improvement in projects and products, leading to better outcomes. Therefore, weaving quantitative and qualitative metrics into your goal-setting framework is essential to create a comprehensive evaluation that reflects the true impact of your team's efforts, instilling confidence in the evaluation process—e impact of your team's efforts.

Balancing Short-Term and Long-Term Goals

Understanding the delicate balance between immediate project deliverables and long-term strategic objectives is a cornerstone of effective software engineering management. While short-term goals drive progress, long-term goals provide a roadmap for sustainable growth. Striking the right balance between these two dimensions is crucial to prevent getting caught up in short-lived tasks and losing sight of broader horizons.

The Art of Balance:

Short-term goals are like the fuel that propels a rocket into space, while long-term goals are the trajectory that ensures it reaches its destination. Just as a rocket needs both to succeed, so does your team. By balancing both dimensions, your team can adapt to changing market conditions without losing sight of long-term success. Therefore, by skillfully coordinating short-term and long-term goals, you can orchestrate a symphony that captures the urgency of the present while keeping an eye on the future.

Combining operational excellence and tech debt reduction with feature work is necessary to ensure any product or service's long-term success and sustainability. Operational excellence ensures that business processes and systems are efficient, effective, and reliable. Tech debt reduction, on the other hand, guarantees that the technology stack is up-to-date, maintainable, and scalable. Neglecting these aspects can lead to technical debt, which can be costly and time-consuming to fix in the future. Therefore, integrating operational excellence and tech debt reduction with feature work ensures that the product or service is functional, efficient, reliable, and maintainable over time, which is crucial for the success of any business.

Regular review and adaptation are essential in the fast-paced world of software engineering. Setting goals is not a one-time event but an ongoing process that requires constant review and adaptation. The industry's rapid pace, changing market dynamics, and unforeseen challenges demand that goals remain in sync with the tempo of change. Regular reviews and adjustments help keep your team on track, allowing you to refine the melody of your goals as needed.

The process of adaptation involves several key elements:

Market Agility: Regular reviews ensure your goals align with shifting market conditions and emerging opportunities.

Lessons Learned: Adaptations are informed by insights gained from past experiences and successes.

Strategic Flexibility: Regular adjustments demonstrate your team's agility and willingness to embrace change.

In addition to regular reviews and adaptations, it's crucial to remember that frequent changes can sometimes create uncertainty and confusion among team members. As a manager, it's your responsibility to get your team's buy-in and communicate any changes clearly and frequently. This helps ensure everyone is on the same page and that changes are implemented smoothly. Over-communication may seem excessive, but it's better to err on caution and ensure everyone understands the goals and how they relate to the team's overall mission. Doing so helps your team stay focused and motivated as they work towards their objectives.

By conducting regular goal reviews and gracefully adapting to new circumstances, you can keep your team's composition in tune with the ever-changing software industry.

Cascading Goals

Establishing a clear and effective goal-setting system, such as 'cascading goals,' is crucial for an organization's success. However, implementing this system can come with its own set of challenges. For instance, ensuring that high-level objectives are effectively broken down into smaller, more achievable goals for each team and individual within the organization can be complex. It requires a structured approach to goal-setting, where the organization can ensure that everyone is working toward the same objectives and that individual efforts are aligned with the overarching company strategy.

The cascading goal process offers several benefits to organizations. First and foremost, it helps ensure 'top-down alignment' throughout the organization. This means individual efforts align with the company's goals and objectives, and everyone works toward a common purpose. 'Top-down alignment' in this context refers to aligning individual and team goals with the overarching company strategy.

In addition to promoting alignment, cascading goals offer greater clarity and focus for employees at all levels of the organization. By breaking down high-level objectives into smaller, more manageable goals, employees can better understand their role in achieving the company's larger vision. This clarity and focus can increase employee engagement and motivation and improve overall performance, making each individual's contribution feel valued and integral to the company's strategy.

Finally, cascading goals can foster greater motivation and unity within the organization. Employees feel a greater sense of purpose and ownership in their work by setting individual goals that contribute to the collective mission. This promotes teamwork and collaboration and improves overall morale and engagement.

In summary, cascading goals are critical for any organization looking to achieve success and drive growth. Organizations can achieve their goals and realize their full potential by aligning individual efforts with the larger company strategy, providing greater clarity and focus, and fostering employee motivation and unity.

Here's an example of cascading goals around a high-level company objective:

High-Level Company Objective: Increase customer satisfaction by 20% within the next year.

Engineering Department's Goal: Enhance product quality and reliability to improve customer satisfaction.

Cascading Goals for the Engineering Team:

1. Develop and Implement Automated Testing Framework:

    b. Objective: Increase test coverage and reduce bugs in production.

    c. Key Results:

        a. Achieve 90% test coverage for critical features within six months.

        b. Implementing automated testing reduces the average bug resolution time from 3 days to 1 day.

2. Improve Scalability and Performance:

    b. Objective: Ensure the product can handle increased user load without performance degradation.

    c. Key Results:

        a. Optimize database queries to reduce response time by 30% within three months.

        b. Conduct load testing to ensure the system can handle 3x the current user load without issues.

3. Enhance User Experience (UX) and User Interface (UI):

> b. Objective: Improve user satisfaction by making the product more intuitive and visually appealing.
>
> c. Key Results:
>
>> a. Implement a user feedback loop to gather UX/UI improvement suggestions and prioritize them based on impact.
>>
>> b. Based on user feedback, a redesigned UI/UX interface will be released within four months, with a target satisfaction score of 85% or higher.

4. Implement Continuous Integration/Continuous Deployment (CI/CD) Pipeline:

> b. Objective: Streamline development processes to ensure faster and more reliable product releases.
>
> c. Key Results:
>
>> a. Within three months, achieve a 95% automated test pass rate in the CI/CD pipeline.
>>
>> b. Reduce deployment time from 2 hours to 30 minutes by optimizing the CI/CD workflow.

5. Training and Skill Development:

> b. Objective: Enhance team skills to adapt to new technologies and best practices.

c. Key Results:

a. Conduct monthly training sessions on emerging technologies relevant to the team's projects.

b. Within six months, certify at least 80% of the team members in relevant skills (e.g., AWS certification, Agile methodologies).

These cascading goals align with the company's objective of increasing customer satisfaction by focusing on areas directly impacting product quality, reliability, user experience, and development efficiency. Each goal is specific, measurable, achievable, relevant, and time-bound (SMART), ensuring clarity and accountability within the engineering team.

Measuring Progress

As a manager, your role in measuring progress is crucial and integral to the team's success. Your guidance keeps the team on track while working towards your goals. Your role is like a guiding light, ensuring everyone works together. For instance, in a software development project, you can measure progress by tracking the number of features implemented or the number of bugs fixed. Regularly tracking progress under your guidance can help you identify issues, make necessary adjustments, and keep your team on course.

Here are five methods that you can use to measure progress efficiently:

Status Meetings: Regular meetings allow discussion of progress, challenges, and adjustments. Doing so lets you stay on top of your team's progress and make informed decisions.

Progress Reports: Timely reports offer a snapshot of progress and form the basis of informed decisions. They help you track what has been achieved and what still needs to be done.

Project Management Tools: These specialized software and tools provide visibility into milestones and task completion, allowing you to easily track your team's progress. They can also help you assign tasks, set deadlines, and monitor individual and team performance. By using these tools effectively, you can streamline your project management process and ensure everyone is on the same page.

Weekly Business Reviews: Besides regular progress tracking, it's essential to review the team's progress every week. This helps you stay on top of any issues that may arise and make adjustments as needed.

Monthly Business Review: A comprehensive monthly business review can provide an overview of your team's performance.

This can include financial statements, sales figures, and other key metrics that help you understand the health of your business. Reviewing these reports monthly lets you identify trends and make data-driven decisions to improve your team's performance.

Importance of Consistency

Consistency is essential for measuring progress and achieving success. Setting regular meeting schedules, submitting timely progress reports, and consistently using project management tools create a rhythm that keeps everyone on the same page. Consistency also helps build trust and accountability within your team, which is critical to driving progress and achieving your goals.

When everyone in the team works towards the same goals and follows the same procedures, it's not just about individual efforts but the collective effort. This collective effort makes it easier to identify areas for improvement and make necessary adjustments. Implementing these methods can ensure that your team works together effectively and that your efforts are in sync. This will help you succeed and build a culture of excellence that drives results, making each team member feel united and part of a shared purpose.

Ultimately, consistency is the key to success in any endeavor. Adopting best practices and sticking to them consistently ensures that your team is aligned and focused on achieving your goals. Whether working on a complex software project or pursuing a personal goal, consistency is the key to success and meaningful progress.

Communication and Transparency

Effective communication and transparency are essential to achieving goals and ensuring harmony among team members. Openly communicating goals transparently fosters a sense of unity, shared purpose, and collective commitment. By engaging in open discussions about progress, challenges, and adjustments, team members can collaborate effectively and achieve success. Feedback is a crucial part of this process. It allows team members to share their thoughts, ideas, and concerns, and it provides a valuable opportunity for learning and growth. By encouraging and valuing feedback, you can create a culture of open communication and transparency that leads to better outcomes for everyone.

The Benefits of Effective Communication

Creating a shared vision is not just a goal; it's a journey that requires open communication and transparency in goal-setting. When team members are transparent and accountable for their commitments, they feel motivated to focus on their responsibilities. Effective communication is the bridge that fosters an environment where everyone understands their role in the collective mission, creating a sense of unity and shared purpose. By conducting open and transparent communication, each team member can contribute uniquely to the team's success, feeling connected and part of something bigger.

Handling Changing Priorities

Priorities can change rapidly. Market trends, customer needs, and internal requirements can alter the direction of your team's efforts. Adapting to these changes with grace and strategic agility allows you to achieve your goals and minimize disruption. Strategic agility is the ability to quickly and effectively respond to changes in the business environment. It involves being proactive, flexible, and innovative in your approach to change. By understanding these challenges, you can take steps to support your team through those challenges and maintain productivity and morale.

Strategies for Adapting:

Flexibility: Be open to changes and view them as opportunities to realign goals and seize new possibilities. Every change is a new opportunity, just as every challenge is a chance to learn.

Open Communication: Communicating the reasons behind changes is crucial for building trust and buy-in from stakeholders. When people understand why a change is necessary or beneficial, they are more likely to support it and work towards its success. Additionally, clear communication can help alleviate concerns or confusion during change, reducing resistance and promoting a smoother transition. Open communication fosters a culture of transparency and collaboration, leading to better outcomes for everyone involved.

Resource Allocation: Reallocate resources according to the revised priorities, optimizing efficiency. When starting a new project, selecting the right team of engineers is crucial to ensure its success. One way to make a new project a win is by identifying engineers who may want to take on new challenges or offer to work with more senior engineers. This can help create a motivated and dedicated team committed to achieving the project goals. Additionally, involving more experienced engineers in the project can bring valuable knowledge and expertise to the team, which can help to ensure that the project is completed to a high standard. When priorities change, it's important to reassess your resources and ensure they align with the new goals. This might involve shifting team members to different projects, hiring new staff, or outsourcing certain tasks.

By mastering the art of handling changing priorities, you can lead your team through the ever-changing landscape of software engineering with confidence and resilience.

Recognition and Celebration

Recognizing and celebrating milestones in big and small goals is more than a formality. It's a powerful gesture that can boost team morale, reinforce a culture of accomplishment, and inspire even more success.

Celebrating achievements can positively impact team morale, fostering a sense of accomplishment and promoting a culture where hard work, dedication, and success are valued. Such celebrations can also motivate team members to continue striving for excellence and promote unity among team members.

By taking the time to orchestrate moments of recognition and celebration, you can show your team that their hard work is appreciated and create an environment where every achievement is a cause for applause.

PERFORMANCE MANAGEMENT

Performance management is a critical and constantly changing process in software engineering management that significantly impacts team success, growth, and excellence. As a manager, you must evaluate and enhance team performance by ensuring that individual efforts align with the team's collective goals. In the previous chapter, we learned that clear and measurable objectives, which are essential for effective performance management, must be defined to achieve this. It's also crucial to reiterate that your team needs well-defined goals and standards to understand their roles in achieving team objectives. Setting expectations gives your team members a clear path to guide their actions.

Setting Expectations

To succeed in any project, it is essential to set clear expectations. For instance, in a software development project, setting the expectation that all new features should undergo automated code reviews can help ensure code quality. By doing so, everyone involved will better understand what is expected of them, their goals, and what they need to do to achieve them. In this regard, there are various approaches that you can use to set expectations effectively. These include collaborative goal-setting, using the SMART framework, and aligning individual and team goals.

Collaborative Goal-Setting: Empowering team members to define their goals is a potent strategy for promoting ownership and commitment. When team members have a voice in setting their goals, they feel a stronger sense of ownership over the outcomes. This motivates them and encourages them to engage actively in the goal-achievement process. Collaborative goal-setting fosters a sense of autonomy, accountability, and shared responsibility within the team. It also allows team members to provide valuable insights and feedback, contributing to more well-rounded and realistic goals.

SMART Framework: The SMART framework stands for Specific, Measurable, Achievable, Relevant, and Time-bound, providing a structured and clear approach to goal-setting. Specific goals are unambiguous, making understanding what needs to be achieved easier. Measurable goals include concrete metrics that allow progress tracking. Achievable goals are realistic and attainable, preventing frustration or demotivation. Relevant goals are aligned with the team's and organization's objectives, ensuring that efforts contribute to broader success. Time-bound goals have well-defined deadlines, creating a sense of urgency. The SMART framework enhances goal clarity and achievability, guiding team members toward success while reducing ambiguity and misunderstandings.

Alignment with Team Goals: Individual goals should align with the team's broader objectives to create a unified sense of direction and purpose. When team members understand how their contributions connect to the larger team goals, it fosters a more cohesive and motivated work environment. It eliminates the siloed approach to goal-setting, where individual objectives may inadvertently conflict with the team's goals. Instead, alignment ensures that team members' efforts are channeled toward a common direction, promoting collaboration and teamwork. This connection between individual and team goals reinforces the notion that the team's success is the sum of its individual members' accomplishments. It also enables a more efficient allocation of resources and a clearer sense of shared responsibility.

Here's an example of a SMART goal for a software engineer:

Goal: *Improve code quality by implementing automated code reviews for all new features in the next quarter.*

Specific: This goal is specific because it outlines what needs to be achieved: implementing automated code reviews for new features.

Measurable: The goal is measurable as success can be tracked through metrics such as the number of automated code reviews conducted and the reduction in post-release bug reports.

Achievable: The goal is achievable because the necessary tools and resources, such as code review software and training, are available within the organization. Given the available means, it's a realistic objective. Setting realistic goals is crucial as it prevents frustration or demotivation that can arise from setting unattainable goals. It also ensures that the team's efforts are focused on goals that can be realistically achieved, contributing to overall project success.

Relevant: Improving code quality is highly relevant to the software engineering team's broader goals of delivering high-quality software and enhancing customer satisfaction.

Time-bound: The goal has a clear timeframe – within the next quarter. This sets a deadline, creating a sense of urgency and providing a timeframe for assessing progress. Deadlines are crucial in goal-setting as they create a sense of urgency and help team members manage their time effectively. They also provide a clear timeframe for assessing progress, allowing for timely adjustments and ensuring the goal is achieved within the desired timeframe.

By adhering to the SMART framework, this goal is well-defined and structured for clarity, making it an effective target for a software engineer to work toward.

Performance Reviews

Regular performance reviews, which you as a manager play a crucial role in facilitating, provide valuable checkpoints for assessing progress, identifying strengths, and addressing areas for improvement. These reviews serve as a platform for meaningful discussions about achievements, challenges, and career aspirations. Your guidance in these conversations is instrumental in helping team members reach their potential.

Approaches for Effective Reviews:

Scheduled Conversations: Conduct regular one-on-one performance reviews at predetermined intervals to track progress over time.

Two-Way Dialogue: Foster a collaborative environment by encouraging team members to share their thoughts and insights during reviews. Use open-ended questions to promote active discussion, ensuring that everyone's voice is heard and valued.

Feedback Collection: Collect feedback from peers and stakeholders through structured surveys or informal conversations to comprehensively view an individual's performance.

Providing Constructive Feedback

Constructive feedback is a cornerstone of performance management. As a manager, you hold the power to guide growth by providing feedback that highlights strengths and suggests areas for improvement. Feedback should be delivered with empathy, respect, and a focus on growth rather than criticism.

Guidelines for Giving Feedback:

Balanced Approach: Acknowledge accomplishments and strengths before discussing areas that need improvement.

Specificity: Provide specific examples to illustrate points and make feedback actionable.

Future Focus: Frame feedback in a way that suggests ways to improve moving forward. Focus on solutions rather than dwelling on past mistakes. This approach encourages a growth mindset and helps team members see feedback as a tool for improvement, not a critique of past performance.

Performance Improvement

While acknowledging accomplishments is essential, addressing performance issues is equally important. As a manager, your role extends to helping team members overcome challenges and supporting them in achieving their best performance. Constructive feedback and targeted coaching are critical components of performance improvement.

One effective way to avoid reaching the point of performance management discussions is by using the Situational Leadership Matrix. This model emphasizes adapting your leadership style to the developmental needs of your team members. By doing so, you can proactively address performance issues before they escalate.

Implementing strategies for performance improvement within the workplace is important. One effective approach is to develop individualized plans for each team member. This involves fostering a collaborative environment by jointly creating improvement plans tailored to each individual's unique needs and areas for growth. By involving team members in the process, you can ensure that the improvement plans are personalized and practical.

In addition to individualized plans, coaching, and mentorship play crucial roles in enhancing team members' skills and addressing performance gaps. Providing guidance and support can help team members overcome challenges and improve their performance. Regular coaching and mentorship opportunities can create a supportive environment for ongoing skill development.

Monitoring the progress of improvement plans is equally important. Continuous tracking allows for regular feedback, which can be instrumental in acknowledging positive changes and addressing any obstacles. By providing consistent support and recognizing improvements as they occur, you can motivate team members to remain committed to their personal and professional growth.

Performance Improvement Plans

A performance improvement plan is a comprehensive document to assist employees in addressing and rectifying performance issues. It consists of several key elements:

Performance Issues: The performance plan, developed through a fair and objective process, should include a clear and specific description of the performance problems and examples of situations where the employee's performance was inadequate. These issues are identified through performance reviews and feedback from multiple sources. The plan should also incorporate objective metrics or standards that were not met.

Performance Improvement Goals: This section should outline specific, measurable, achievable, relevant, and time-bound (SMART) goals. SMART goals are designed to be clear and specific, allowing easy tracking and measuring progress. They are also realistic and achievable, ensuring the employee is not overwhelmed. The goals should define detailed expectations and standards the employee needs to meet and establish clear deadlines for achieving these goals. Understanding the concept of SMART goals is crucial as it helps the employee to set realistic and achievable targets, making their performance improvement journey more effective.

Action Plan: The action plan should include detailed steps the employee will take to improve performance. It may involve training and development activities such as courses, workshops, seminars, and mentorship and coaching opportunities, such as pairing with a senior employee. Additionally, it should specify the resources and tools provided to support improvement, such as software for data analysis, books on effective communication, and access to online learning platforms.

Monitoring and Feedback: This part of the plan should outline a schedule for regular check-ins and progress reviews, such as weekly or bi-weekly meetings. These meetings are a key part of the plan and are designed to provide ongoing feedback and support to the employee. They allow for a continuous assessment of the employee's progress and provide an opportunity to make any necessary adjustments to the plan. The plan should also elucidate the methods for providing feedback, including meetings or written reports. Furthermore, it should establish criteria for evaluating progress and adjusting the plan as necessary, such as meeting specific performance targets or demonstrating improvement in key areas.

Support and Resources: The performance plan should highlight the extensive support from the manager and the organization. It should also emphasize the employee's unrestricted access to training materials, tools, and professional development resources, as well as the unwavering encouragement and assistance from team members or mentors.

Consequences of Not Meeting Goals: This portion should give a clear and fair explanation of the consequences if performance does not improve. It should outline potential outcomes, such as further training to address specific areas of improvement, reassignment to a different role that better aligns with the employee's skills, or, in extreme cases, termination. These outcomes are not meant to be punitive but to ensure that the employee's performance aligns with the organization's expectations. The plan should also establish a timeline for re-evaluation and decision-making, providing a clear path forward.

At the end of the specified review period, there should be a summary of the progress made, notes on any adjustments to the plan, and an outline of the next steps or further actions required.

Incorporating these elements into a performance improvement plan ensures its comprehensiveness and clarity and emphasizes its supportive nature. It provides the employee with a structured path, guiding them towards enhancing their performance and meeting organizational expectations. However, it's important to note that the plan's success ultimately depends on the employee's commitment and active participation. Their willingness to engage in the process and make the necessary changes is crucial for the plan's effectiveness.

DEALING WITH CHALLENGES

As a software engineering manager, you oversee the development and delivery of complex software systems. This role can be demanding due to challenges such as managing conflicting priorities, balancing technical debt with project timelines, and navigating resource constraints.

As a software engineering manager, your role in team dynamics is not just important; it's pivotal. You are the linchpin that can effectively manage them, an essential role for our collective success. Your ability to identify and address conflicts within the team, encourage open communication, and build a culture of trust is what holds us together. Without your guidance, a cohesive team can quickly fall apart. Your contribution to the team's success is invaluable.

As a software engineering manager, you wield the authority to plan project timelines effectively. This is not just important; it's crucial, as you are constantly under pressure to meet tight deadlines. Your skill in allocating resources efficiently and managing scope changes as they arise can prevent missed opportunities, keep clients happy, and ensure revenue is not lost. Your authority in this area gives you the power to steer the project toward success.

Technical debt constantly threatens to derail even the most well-planned projects. As a software engineering manager, you must ensure that technical debt is managed effectively so it doesn't burden future projects. This includes regular code reviews, refactoring, and maintaining a high level of code quality.

Finally, resource constraints can make your job more difficult. However, as a software engineering manager, you can effectively manage your team's workload, ensuring they have the resources to do their jobs while staying within budget constraints. Your capability in this area is a testament to your skills and experience.

In this chapter, we will cover all of these points in detail and provide you with strategies and techniques to mitigate risks associated with software engineering management. We will start by discussing the challenges of team dynamics, then move on to the strategies for meeting tight deadlines, managing technical debt, and dealing with resource constraints. By the end of this chapter, you will better understand the challenges and opportunities that come with this role and be equipped with the tools you need to succeed.

Getting Comfortable With Uncertainty

In software engineering, achieving operational excellence requires focusing on risk management and resilience. Risk management involves identifying potential challenges and implementing strategies to prevent or mitigate them. It is akin to seeing around corners and predicting future problems before they occur. This section emphasizes the importance of risk management in achieving and maintaining operational excellence, highlighting the significance of preparedness and the development of resilience.

Embracing Resilience in the Face of Uncertainty

Resilience is the anchor that keeps a ship steady during turbulent times. Similarly, resilience in software engineering allows teams to weather unexpected challenges with poise and recover gracefully. It involves building systems and processes that can adapt to changing conditions and recover from disruptions.

Adaptability: Resilient systems and teams can adapt to unexpected changes, ensuring ongoing progress.

Swift Recovery: Resilience enables teams to recover from setbacks quickly and efficiently.

The Role of Contingency Planning

Tabletop exercises are also valuable tools for contingency planning. These exercises simulate potential disruptions and allow teams to practice implementing their contingency plans in a safe environment. This helps identify any weaknesses in the plan and improve response times.

Amazon, for instance, has a well-established operational readiness review process that includes tabletop exercises. This process involves regularly reviewing and testing contingency plans to ensure they are up-to-date and effective, helping the company respond quickly and efficiently to unexpected disruptions.

Overall, contingency planning and regular testing, using tools like tabletop exercises and operational readiness reviews, are crucial for any team to ensure they can respond effectively to unforeseen challenges.

In addition to tabletop exercises and operational readiness reviews, another valuable technique for identifying potential problems before they escalate is using "canaries." Canaries are small and safe tests performed regularly to detect potential issues before they escalate into larger problems that can impact customers.

The canaries involve running small-scale tests in a controlled environment to identify potential issues before they affect customers. For example, canaries can test new software updates or changes to a website's functionality before they are released to the public. By running these tests in a controlled environment, teams can identify problems and make necessary fixes before customers are affected.

By regularly running canaries, teams can detect and resolve potential problems before they escalate into more significant issues that can impact customers. This approach ensures that potential problems are detected and resolved before they cause significant disruptions.

In conclusion, adding the concept of canaries to contingency planning and regular testing through tools like tabletop exercises and operational readiness reviews can help teams detect and resolve potential issues before customers are impacted. This approach ensures teams respond effectively to unforeseen challenges and provide customers with a seamless experience.

Creating a Culture of Preparedness

Risk management and resilience cannot be considered in isolation; they are important components that contribute to a culture of preparedness. Similar to how a ship's crew undergoes emergency drills, teams prioritizing risk management foster a culture where they face challenges with preparation, adaptability, and collective action.

Shared responsibility is vital: A culture of preparedness ensures that every team member understands their role in mitigating risks. This means everyone takes responsibility and contributes to risk management's collective effort.

Quick responses are crucial: Prepared teams can respond quickly to challenges, preventing them from worsening. This helps to prevent the situation from escalating and causing more harm.

Conclusion

Risk management and resilience are important components of achieving operational excellence in software engineering. Teams prioritizing risk management are better equipped to handle challenges, prevent potential issues, and build resilience in uncertainty. By promoting a culture of preparedness, organizations can ensure that their operational excellence remains strong enough to withstand disruptions and continue making steady progress toward their goals.

Change Management

Introducing change is an inevitable part of any team or project. However, it can be challenging to bring about changes without facing some resistance from the team members. The resistance may arise for various reasons, such as fear of the unknown, lack of understanding, or concerns about how the changes might impact their roles.

To mitigate these concerns and ensure a smoother transition, managers must take a proactive approach to change management. This involves providing clear communication and actively involving team members throughout the process. By doing so, managers can help team members understand the changes, why they are necessary, and how they will impact the team.

One of the most important aspects of effective change management is providing context. Team members must know why the changes are necessary and how they fit into the team or project's overall strategy. This will help them better understand their work's impact on the project's success and the organization's goals.

Another crucial step is to actively seek and value team members' feedback. By asking for their input, managers can address any concerns and identify potential issues that may arise during the transition process. This will also help team members feel more engaged and valued, which can help reduce resistance to change.

Finally, fostering a culture of adaptability is not just a necessity but an exciting opportunity. Change is a constant in today's fast-paced business world, and teams must be ready to adapt to new processes, technologies, and methodologies. This means creating an environment where team members feel comfortable challenging the status quo and proposing new ideas. By doing so, managers can empower their teams to embrace changes and

JOSHUAMCDONALD

drive innovation.

Scope Creep and Managing Expectations

Scope creep is a common problem affecting any project, including engineering projects. As an engineering manager, your role is crucial in ensuring that projects are completed on time, within budget, and to the satisfaction of all stakeholders. However, scope creep can make this problematic as requirements change and additional features are requested. If not managed effectively, scope creep can lead to project delays, budget overruns, and stakeholder dissatisfaction, significantly impacting the project's success. Your expertise and leadership are key in navigating these challenges.

Effective communication is key for engineering managers in their efforts to manage scope creep. It involves setting realistic timelines, budgets, and deliverables. When a stakeholder proposes an additional feature or a change in the project scope, the engineering manager should assess the impact of this change on the project timeline and budget. If the change is viable, the manager can negotiate a new deadline or budget with the stakeholders, fostering understanding and collaboration for better project outcomes.

If the change is not feasible, it's important to stand firm and explain why it cannot be accommodated. For instance, if a stakeholder requests a new feature requiring significant additional resources, you can elucidate the impact this would have on the project timeline and budget. However, you can also propose a more realistic alternative solution, reassuring the reader about the possibility of finding a way forward even in challenging situations. Your expertise and problem-solving skills are instrumental in this process.

Managing scope creep often requires tough decision-making. For instance, if a stakeholder requests an additional feature that is not feasible within the current budget or timeline, the engineering manager may need to suggest removing another feature or reducing the project scope. This demonstrates leadership and ensures that the project remains aligned with its goals and objectives, even in the face of scope creep.

In summary, managing scope creep requires a proactive approach, effective communication, and a willingness to make tough decisions when necessary. By setting clear boundaries, managing expectations, and negotiating trade-offs, engineering managers can ensure that their projects stay on track and meet the needs of all stakeholders.

Stakeholder Management

Stakeholders, including clients, team members, sponsors, end-users, and regulatory bodies, are not just participants in a project ecosystem but integral contributors to its success. To effectively manage stakeholder engagement, it is crucial to recognize their diverse perspectives, interests, and influence levels. Conducting a thorough stakeholder analysis early in the project lifecycle can help managers gain insights into stakeholders' expectations, concerns, and communication preferences. This allows for tailored engagement approaches that foster constructive dialogue and mutual understanding, making each stakeholder feel valued and integral to the project's success.

Establishing clear communication channels catering to each stakeholder group's unique needs is crucial to successful stakeholder engagement. This can be achieved through regular progress meetings, status reports, or digital platforms. Managers can foster an environment of transparency and collaboration by maintaining an open-door policy and actively seeking feedback. Transparent expectation management, which involves setting realistic expectations about timelines, budgets, and deliverables, is key to building trust and credibility with stakeholders. It also involves proactively communicating potential roadblocks, changes, and trade-offs, helping stakeholders understand the project's constraints and potential challenges.

Soliciting and incorporating stakeholder feedback is not just a process, but a critical aspect of iterative project management and continuous improvement. By actively seeking stakeholder input at key milestones and touchpoints, managers can identify pain points, address emerging issues, and fine-tune project strategies to better align with stakeholder priorities. Managers can also galvanize stakeholders to actively participate in problem-solving and decision-making by fostering a culture of constructive feedback and shared ownership, making each stakeholder feel heard and appreciated.

Strong stakeholder relationships are built on consistent value delivery and outcomes that exceed expectations. Managers can instill confidence and loyalty among stakeholders by relentlessly focusing on quality, innovation, and customer satisfaction. Celebrating achievements, recognizing contributions, and acknowledging lessons learned along the journey can reinforce a culture of appreciation and shared success, fostering enduring partnerships that transcend individual projects.

Technical Debt

Technical debt, a common challenge in software development, can be best understood through real-life examples. Imagine a scenario where a team, under pressure to meet a deadline, implements a quick fix for a bug they know is not the best solution. This decision, while solving the immediate problem, incurs a debt. Over time, this debt can accumulate and ultimately affect project progress, leading to increased maintenance costs, decreased productivity, and even project failure.

To maintain project health, teams must balance short-term needs with long-term code quality and refactoring efforts. This means teams should set aside time in their roadmaps to address technical debt. By doing so, they can prevent the accumulation of technical debt, which, if left unattended, can lead to increased maintenance costs, decreased productivity, and even project failure. Addressing technical debt ensures that the codebase remains maintainable and scalable over time, safeguarding the project's success and the team's productivity.

Managers play a pivotal role in addressing technical debt. They are responsible for prioritizing its reduction, strategically allocating resources, and fostering a culture of code quality within the team. This involves not just promoting code reviews, testing, and refactoring, but also providing training and resources to keep developers updated with best practices and new technologies. By emphasizing this role, managers can feel empowered and responsible for the team's code quality, leading to more effective technical debt management.

Managers should not rely solely on their judgment when determining which technical debt to prioritize. Instead, they can implement strategies such as conducting regular code reviews, engaging in open discussions with the development team, and using tools that analyze code quality. This approach ensures that the team's efforts are aligned with the most pressing needs and makes engineers feel valued and integral to the process, ultimately leading to more effective technical debt management.

In summary, addressing technical debt is essential for maintaining project health. By building time into roadmaps, prioritizing technical debt reduction, allocating resources strategically, and fostering a code quality culture, teams can deliver sustainable, maintainable, and scalable solutions.

As an engineering manager, it's crucial to remember that your role extends beyond delivering features and products. Ensuring their operational soundness is equally important. Overemphasizing one aspect over the other can lead to team failure. Therefore, maintaining a balance between the two is not just key but urgent and crucial to the project's success. This balance keeps the team's work sustainable and the solutions maintainable and scalable, ensuring the long-term success of the project.

In conclusion, software engineering management is fraught with challenges, but with the right strategies and mindset, managers can overcome obstacles and foster growth and innovation within their teams. For example, managers can prioritize communication by implementing regular team meetings and using collaboration tools to ensure everyone is on the same page. They can foster collaboration by encouraging cross-functional teams and providing knowledge-sharing opportunities. They can also promote continuous learning by organizing training sessions and providing resources for self-study. By prioritizing these strategies, managers can empower their teams to thrive in an ever-changing landscape of technology and business demands and effectively manage technical debt.

OPERATIONAL EXCELLENCE

Pursuing and maintaining excellence in software engineering is not a fleeting endeavor but a mindset that must be fostered and honed over time. It's not merely about good intentions but about the mechanisms and processes you, as software engineers and team leaders, implement. Your role is pivotal, as you are the ones propelling your team toward greatness. This chapter is dedicated to instilling a mindset that consistently delivers superior results, thrives on continuous improvement, and steers your team toward excellence through effective mechanisms.

Operational excellence in software engineering is not just a mindset but an approach that consistently yields high-quality results while continually improving processes for maximum efficiency and effectiveness. This approach is not a solitary endeavor but a collaborative one that involves all team members infusing the pursuit of excellence into every aspect of software engineering, from coding and testing to deployment and maintenance. It's about meeting or surpassing stakeholder expectations, making it a vital component of software engineering.

Operational excellence in software engineering necessitates

establishing streamlined workflows and promoting efficient collaboration. It's a mindset of constantly searching for ways to enhance processes, reduce waste, and optimize resources for maximum efficiency and effectiveness. Rest assured, this is not an impossible challenge but a continuous journey of improvement. With your leadership, you can steer your team toward operational excellence by relentlessly pursuing excellence in every endeavor.

Achieving operational excellence is a continuous process that requires a dedicated mindset and approach to deliver superior results consistently. By adopting this approach and integrating it into every aspect of software engineering, you can ensure your team strives to achieve greatness and deliver the best possible outcomes for stakeholders. These outcomes, including faster market time, higher-quality products, and improved customer satisfaction, are not just benefits but also inspirations for your team to keep pushing for excellence.

Operational excellence in software engineering comprises several aspects, each essential in ensuring successful project delivery. High-quality results are critical to operational excellence, ensuring the output meets the highest quality standards. This includes functional correctness, meaning the output is tested and verified to meet the intended functionality. Additionally, aspects like code readability, maintainability, and scalability must be considered to ensure that the output can be easily maintained and scaled up as required.

Consistency is another vital aspect characterized by the reliable delivery of outcomes. The team strives to minimize process variations and unpredictability to build trust with stakeholders and users. Ensuring that the output is delivered on time, within budget, and meets the required quality standards is crucial for maintaining this trust and ensuring consistent delivery.

The essence of operational excellence lies in the commitment to continuous improvement. Teams that embody operational excellence always seek opportunities to optimize processes, reduce waste, and enhance efficiency over time. This involves identifying areas for improvement, devising and implementing strategies to address them, and measuring the effectiveness of these solutions to ensure they meet the desired outcomes. It's a journey of perpetual learning and growth.

Efficient workflows are synonymous with operational excellence. This includes identifying bottlenecks, eliminating unnecessary steps, and automating routine tasks to facilitate smoother collaboration and faster results. By optimizing workflows, teams can reduce lead times, improve productivity, minimize errors, and enhance efficiency and outcomes.

Proactive problem-solving is also a key element. Teams practicing operational excellence adopt a proactive stance toward identifying and addressing issues. They actively seek out potential problems before they escalate and disrupt progress, develop and implement strategies to address potential issues, regularly assess risks, and take corrective action as required.

Finally, data-driven decision-making is essential within an operationally excellent culture. Decisions are based on empirical evidence and insights, reducing the reliance on gut feelings and assumptions. Teams collect and analyze data to gain insights into performance, identify areas for improvement, and make informed decisions that lead to better outcomes.

By integrating these aspects into every part of their work, software engineering teams can achieve operational excellence, ultimately driving faster time to market, higher quality products, and improved customer satisfaction.

In summary, operational excellence in software engineering is a multifaceted approach that involves a dedicated mindset, consistent, high-quality results, continuous improvement, efficient workflows, proactive problem-solving, and data-driven decision-making. Integrating these aspects into every part of your work can lead your team to achieve superior outcomes, ultimately driving faster time to market, higher quality products, and improved customer satisfaction.

Setting the Tone

In the ever-evolving realm of software engineering, leaders guide their team's performance and chart the course to success. They are responsible for fostering a culture of excellence that breeds positive outcomes. Exceptional leaders profoundly understand the software development process and can effectively communicate their vision and expectations to their team. They set the tone for the entire team, creating an environment that nurtures collaboration, encourages creativity, and instills a continuous improvement mindset, boosting team morale and motivation. This can be done through various means, such as leading by example, providing clear and consistent communication, and creating opportunities for team members to learn and grow. By setting the right tone, leaders can create a positive work environment that fosters a culture of excellence and drives the team toward success.

Through their leadership, they develop a cohesive team that can seamlessly work towards common goals. They establish clear communication channels, crucial in overcoming obstacles and challenges. Leaders play a pivotal role in identifying these hurdles, devising strategies to overcome them, and ensuring their team is equipped with the necessary resources and tools to succeed. They also provide guidance and support when necessary, fostering a culture of resilience and continuous improvement.

In essence, a great leader in software engineering is not just a manager but a mentor, coach, and guide. They inspire their team to achieve their best work, lead by example, and cultivate a culture of excellence that is critical to the success of any software development project. By taking on the mentor role, leaders guide and make their team members feel valued and supported, fostering a sense of belonging and commitment.

Leading by Example

Being a leader is about holding a position and embodying the values and behaviors you wish to see in your team. Leaders are the soloists on the stage, demonstrating the standards of excellence they expect from their team members through their actions. For instance, a leader who consistently meets deadlines maintains a positive attitude even in challenging situations and actively seeks feedback from team members, setting a high standard for their team. When leaders consistently exhibit a dedication to quality, attention to detail, and improvement, they inspire others to follow suit.

One example of leading by example is a manager who always arrives to work on time, works diligently, and maintains a positive attitude. By doing so, the manager sets the standard for punctuality, work ethic, and attitude for their team members. As a result, their team members are more likely to follow suit and exhibit the same behaviors and values. Additionally, if the manager constantly seeks feedback and strives to improve themselves, team members will be motivated to do the same.

Consistency is a crucial element of leading by example. When leaders consistently exhibit the behaviors and values they wish to see in their team members, it sends a clear message that those behaviors and values are essential and expected. On the other hand, if a leader only occasionally exhibits those behaviors or values, it can be unclear and demotivating for team members. Consistency also helps build trust and credibility with team members. When team members see that their leader is consistently committed to improvement and growth, they are more likely to trust their leader's guidance and follow their example. Therefore, leaders should consciously try to consistently embody the behaviors and values they wish to see in their team members.

Modeling Behavior

Effective leaders who consistently demonstrate a strong work ethic by putting in the time and effort required to achieve success, paying attention to even the smallest details, and relentlessly pursuing excellence set a high standard for their team members to emulate. In software engineering, this means showing dedication to writing clean code, conducting thorough testing, and continuously learning and improving. By modeling these qualities, leaders create a culture of excellence that inspires their team members to work diligently, pay attention to details, and strive for excellence in all their endeavors. This culture of excellence drives the team to achieve outstanding results and fosters a sense of pride and accomplishment in team members.

Communicating the Importance of Quality

Effective communication is crucial in software engineering projects, as it ensures that everyone is aligned with the project goals and working together in harmony. To achieve excellence in software engineering, leaders must play a crucial role in emphasizing the significance of quality and clear and consistent communication.

High-quality results are not just a task but a fundamental principle that underpins the entire team's success. Leaders must communicate this message clearly and consistently, ensuring every team member understands the importance of producing high-quality results. This can be done through various means, such as team meetings, one-on-one discussions, or the team's communication channels. By consistently emphasizing the importance of quality, leaders can instill this value in their team and drive them towards excellence.

Clear communication is the cornerstone of successful software engineering projects. It ensures everyone is on the same page, working efficiently towards the same goal. This includes communicating project timelines, milestones, and any potential roadblocks or challenges that may arise during the project lifecycle. Effective communication also involves actively listening to team members, addressing their concerns and feedback, and providing support and guidance. By emphasizing the importance of clear communication, leaders ensure efficient work and make their team members feel understood and involved, fostering a sense of unity and shared responsibility.

Attention to detail and clear communication are critical in software engineering projects. Leaders must encourage their team members to work precisely and accurately, ensuring that every aspect of the project is thoroughly reviewed and tested before delivery. This helps eliminate any potential bugs or errors in the final product.

In conclusion, effective communication, attention to detail, and a focus on producing high-quality results are essential to achieving excellence in software engineering projects. Leaders are critical in emphasizing these principles and ensuring that every team member is aligned with these goals, resulting in successful project outcomes.

Quality as a Core Value

Leaders should weave quality into the fabric of the team's identity, making it a non-negotiable core value that guides all actions and decisions. In software engineering, this means ensuring that every line of code, every feature, and every product meets the highest quality standards. One way to accomplish this is to ensure that your team's 'tenets, 'or guiding principles, reflect the drive toward operational excellence. An example tenet may be :

Accuracy and precision are table stakes - we will sacrifice time and treasure to ensure that our code is consistently defect-free.

In my experience, this tenant usually sits at the top under security as a guiding principle for the team.

Defining operational metrics, a task that leaders are uniquely positioned to do is crucial to successful software engineering projects. These metrics help measure the project's progress and provide valuable insights into the team's performance. By setting clear and achievable metrics, leaders can motivate their team members to work towards the same goal, ensuring everyone is aligned with the project's objectives.

Regular meetings are a key responsibility of leaders. They allow team members to discuss progress, share ideas, and provide feedback. These meetings serve as a platform for team members to align their efforts, review project milestones, identify potential roadblocks, and discuss solutions to any challenges. Leaders must ensure that these meetings are productive and efficient, with a clear agenda, timeline, and action items. By conducting effective meetings, leaders can keep their team on track and ensure everyone is working towards the same goal.

Consistently performing these functions is critical to the project's success. Leaders must monitor progress, provide feedback and guidance, and promptly address issues. This involves closely monitoring the project's timeline, ensuring the team consistently meets its operational metrics, and promptly addressing any issues. By doing so, leaders can ensure that the project stays on track, maintain team morale, and foster a culture of continuous improvement.

Defining operational metrics, holding regular meetings, and consistently performing those functions are essential to achieving excellence in software engineering projects. By emphasizing the importance of these functions, leaders can motivate their team members to work together towards a common goal, resulting in successful project outcomes.

Inspiring Ownership and Accountability

A sense of ownership and accountability can positively impact teamwork and overall performance. Leaders can empower their team members by delegating responsibilities and instilling a sense of ownership in their work. By doing so, individuals are more likely to take pride in their contributions and view each task as an opportunity to contribute to the team's success.

Empowering autonomy by delegating authority and providing more independence can motivate team members to take the initiative and go the extra mile to deliver outstanding results.

Building a Culture of Continuous Improvement

Continuous improvement is essential for achieving operational excellence. To accomplish this, leaders play a critical role in inspiring and motivating their teams. They create a culture where successes are celebrated, setbacks are seen as learning opportunities, and every accomplishment is viewed as a stepping stone toward even greater success.

Encouraging innovation is one of the most crucial ways leaders can foster a culture of growth and development. It involves creating an environment that welcomes experimentation, embraces risk-taking, and sees failures as opportunities to learn and grow. By doing so, leaders can help their teams develop innovative solutions to their challenges, ultimately leading to tremendous success.

To achieve this, managers can organize idea sessions and encourage the creation of one-page documents that describe bottlenecks or pain points in their current architecture. However, to ensure that their teams continue to bring ideas forward, managers should implement a certain number of initiatives every quarter; otherwise, planning sessions may be viewed as just planning without any real action.

Habits That Drive Operational Excellence

Quality assurance and testing are not just necessary in software engineering, they are the pillars of high-quality output. Teams that prioritize these rigorous processes create a culture where excellence is not just a goal, but a standard. This commitment to quality not only ensures customer satisfaction but also boosts team morale and productivity.

Automated Testing

Automated testing is not just a process; it's a game-changer in software development. Using software tools to conduct tests, compare results, and provide feedback helps identify bugs, errors, and other issues before the software is released. This early detection saves time and effort and ensures a smoother user experience.

Automated testing tools simulate user interactions with the software to verify whether the expected response is generated. These tools meticulously evaluate the software's functionalities, ensuring it behaves correctly under various conditions.

One significant advantage of automated testing is that it ensures consistency and efficiency. The same tests can be repeated without variation, providing consistent results and saving time. This consistency also enables developers to compare test results over time and identify any changes in software performance.

Another essential benefit of automated testing is regression testing. This type of testing involves verifying that new changes to the software do not introduce unintended bugs or break existing features. Automated testing can help to catch regressions, which is particularly useful in complex software systems where manual testing is time-consuming and prone to errors.

In summary, automated testing is a powerful and essential tool for software development. It empowers software engineers by ensuring software quality, saving valuable development time, and preventing unintended consequences of software changes.

Code Reviews

Code reviews are not just a formality; they are the key to enhancing the quality of your code. Like melodies that enrich a composition, they offer valuable insights, identify potential issues, and ensure that the code aligns with your team's standards and practices. By making code reviews a regular part of your development process, you can significantly improve the quality of your code.

Additionally, code reviews provide an excellent opportunity for team members to learn from one another and share knowledge. They help catch inconsistencies, improve code readability, and ultimately enhance the overall quality of the code. Some helpful tips for code reviews include:

Establish Clear Guidelines: Define coding standards and best practices and review guidelines that all team members should follow. Well-documented standards help reviewers and developers understand the expectations.

Set Expectations: Communicate the code review's goals and objectives. Are you seeking code quality improvements, security checks, or design feedback? Setting expectations ensures that reviewers focus on the most critical aspects.

Use Code Review Tools: Leverage code review tools and platforms like GitHub, GitLab, or Bitbucket to streamline the review process. These tools provide features like inline comments and version control integration. You want to employ automation as much as possible to remove the need for people to remember to complete a task - at Amazon, it's referred to as mechanisms versus good intentions.

Keep Reviews Small and Focused: It's often more effective to review smaller, manageable pieces of code rather than large chunks. Smaller reviews are easier to understand and less time-consuming. Let your team know it's ok to reject a large pull request.

Review Early and Often: This goes hand in hand with the point above. Encourage early code reviews to catch issues before they become deeply ingrained in the codebase. Frequent, smaller reviews help maintain code quality over time.

Maintain a Constructive Tone: Approach code reviews with a constructive and positive mindset. Focus on improving the code, not criticizing the developer. Use polite and precise language in your comments.

Collaborative Discussions: Encouraging discussions between the author and reviewer is crucial to clarify concerns and reach a consensus on improvements. It is essential to document the different decision points made during these discussions. This documentation can serve as a reference point for both parties, ensuring that they are on the same page and can track the progress of the review process. Documenting these decisions also helps to avoid any confusion or misunderstandings that may arise during the review process. Documenting decision points during discussions can streamline the review process and make it more efficient, fostering a sense of teamwork and collaboration.

Documentation and Comments: Ensure the code is well-documented and the comments are clear and informative. The code should be self-explanatory, and comments should provide additional context where necessary.

Testing and Validation: Verify that the code has been adequately tested and that the tests cover different scenarios. Code reviews are an excellent opportunity to check for test coverage and correctness. Ideally, your team will integrate tests into your CI/CD pipeline so that a PR will fail if any tests fail—that, however, does not mean that there is adequate test coverage. You should encourage engineers to think about the functions being tested and any edge cases that may have been missed.

Follow Up on Feedback: Developers should take feedback seriously and promptly address issues raised during code reviews. Encourage a culture of continuous improvement.

Rotate Reviewers: Rotate team members who participate in code reviews. Different perspectives can lead to a more well-rounded evaluation of the code. In a very small team I once led, we did this by assigning a number to each individual and rolling an 8-sided die. You should also aim to ensure a mix of senior and junior engineers responsible for reviewing code.

Training and Mentorship: Offer training and mentorship for junior team members. Guide code quality, best practices, and how to conduct effective code reviews.

Continuous Improvement: As a software engineering manager, it's crucial to periodically assess the effectiveness of our code review process and make adjustments as needed. It's important to stay up-to-date with changing project requirements and technologies and be able to adapt accordingly. We must ensure that our team produces high-quality work that meets our client's needs and that our code review process is optimized for efficiency and effectiveness. This commitment to continuous improvement inspires our team to strive for better quality in their work.res our team to strive for better quality in their work.

Implementing these tips can help teams conduct more effective code reviews, leading to higher code quality, knowledge sharing, and a more robust, collaborative development environment.

Continuous Integration

Continuous Integration (CI) and Continuous Delivery (CD) are software development practices that help to streamline the development process, making it more efficient and effective.

Continuous Integration frequently integrates code changes into a shared repository. This practice involves automated build and testing processes that help identify and resolve issues early on, resulting in faster feedback and a higher-quality end product. By incorporating code changes more frequently, developers can work more efficiently and reduce the risk of conflicts that can slow down the development process.

Continuous Delivery, on the other hand, is the practice of automating the entire software delivery process, from building and testing to deployment and release. This practice involves continuous changes from development to production, aiming to deliver software to customers more quickly and reliably. By automating the entire process, developers can reduce the risk of errors and increase the speed of delivery.

Imagine a team of developers working on an e-commerce website. Their workflow incorporates CI/CD practices to streamline the development process. Here's how it works:

Code Development and Version Control: Developers write code for new features or bug fixes locally on their machines. They use a version control system like Git to manage changes efficiently. Each developer works on a feature branch, keeping the main branch stable.

Continuous Integration (CI): As developers push their code changes to the remote repository, a CI server (such as Jenkins, Travis CI, or CircleCI) automatically triggers a series of tests against the new code. These tests include unit tests, integration tests, and other quality checks to ensure the code meets the project's standards.

Automated Testing: Once the CI server detects new code changes, it pulls the latest code from the repository and runs the automated test suite. These tests validate the application's functionality and check for any regressions or bugs introduced by the new code. If any tests fail, the CI server notifies the development team, allowing them to address issues promptly.

Code Review and Feedback: Developers initiate a code review process before merging their code into the main branch. Other team members review the proposed changes, provide feedback, and ensure adherence to coding standards and best practices. Code reviews help maintain code quality and prevent issues from being introduced into the codebase.

Continuous Deployment (CD): Once the code changes pass all tests and receive approval through the code review process, they are ready for deployment. The CI/CD pipeline automatically deploys the changes to a staging environment, where they undergo further testing in a production-like environment. This ensures that the application behaves as expected before being released to end-users.

Release to Production: After successful testing in the staging environment, the changes are deployed to the production environment. This deployment process may involve additional checks and safeguards to minimize the risk of disruptions to the live application. Automated rollback mechanisms are in place to revert to the previous version in case of unexpected issues.

Monitoring and Feedback Loop: Once the changes are deployed to production, monitoring tools track the application's performance and stability in real-time. The development team promptly addresses any anomalies or errors, and feedback is used to iterate and improve the CI/CD pipeline for future releases.

Continuous Integration and Continuous Delivery create a seamless software development process that helps teams work more efficiently and effectively. By automating key processes and integrating code changes more frequently, developers can identify and resolve issues earlier, resulting in faster feedback and a higher-quality end product.

Developing a culture of quality

Developing a culture of quality is a challenging task that requires intentional efforts. Teams prioritizing quality assurance and testing communicate that delivering exceptional software is not just a one-time achievement but an ongoing journey. It's a commitment to provide consistently high-quality software.

Every team member, from code developers to testers who conduct tests, plays a critical role in maintaining quality. This collective responsibility ensures everyone is accountable for the final product's quality, leaving no one behind.

Aligning incentives for developers is crucial in promoting a quality culture in software engineering. Rather than solely focusing on the number of commits or lines of code, it's essential to recognize the importance of quality over quantity. Code review is an integral part of the development process, and ensuring that it reflects the company's quality standards is crucial. By aligning incentives with quality, developers will be motivated to prioritize quality over speed, leading to better software and improved user experiences. This approach can also be reflected in the promotion process, where developers prioritizing quality are recognized and rewarded accordingly. Such a culture will encourage developers to take ownership of their work and strive towards delivering high-quality software consistently.

Operational Excellence and OKRs

Operational Excellence is a critical aspect of any business. It is a continuous journey that requires aligning processes and objectives to achieve desired results. Successful companies like Google and Intel use the Objectives and Key Results (OKRs) methodology to achieve this.

An Objective is a specific goal to be achieved within a particular time frame. It should be challenging, inspirational, achievable, aligned with the company's vision and mission, and measurable.

A Key Result is a metric used to measure progress towards achieving the objective. It should be specific, measurable, achievable, relevant, and time-bound. Key Results should also be quantifiable, which means they should have a numerical value attached to them.

Ground rules must be followed to measure the objective's success and key results. First, the Objective and Key Results should be visible and transparent to the organization. Second, progress towards achieving the Objective and Key Results should be regularly tracked and reported. Third, the Objective and Key Results should be reviewed and updated regularly to ensure they remain relevant and aligned with the company's vision and mission.

Google has been using OKRs since its inception in 1999, which has helped it focus on its core objectives and achieve significant growth. Similarly, Intel adopted OKRs in 1971 when they struggled to maintain a competitive edge in the market. The OKRs helped Intel to prioritize and align its efforts, leading to a remarkable turnaround in the company's fortunes.

In conclusion, the OKRs methodology is a powerful tool for achieving operational excellence. It provides a clear direction and helps prioritize tasks, ensuring everyone works towards the same goals. Google and Intel are examples of companies that have successfully adopted and used OKRs to achieve significant growth and success.

An example of an OKR for an engineering team could be:

Objective: Improve the Performance of Our Software Application

Key Results:

Increase the application's loading speed by 30%.

Reduce the number of crashes by 50%.

Achieve a user satisfaction rating of 4.5 stars or higher.

This OKR aligns with the overall goal of delivering high-quality, well-performing software. It provides a clear direction for the engineering team and helps prioritize tasks to achieve the desired results.

An example of a personal OKR could be:

Objective: Improve My Health and Fitness

Key Results:

Exercise for at least 30 minutes daily for the next three months.

Reduce my daily sugar intake to less than 20 grams.

Achieve a weight loss of 10 pounds by the end of the quarter.

This personal OKR aligns with the overall goal of improving health and fitness. It provides a clear direction for personal efforts and helps to prioritize tasks to achieve the desired results.

Mechanisms Versus Good Intentions

Efficiency is vital to achieving operational excellence, which requires more than just intentions. In this context, 'mechanisms' refer to practical tools or processes that help translate aspirations into concrete actions, ensuring the desired outcomes are achieved consistently and reliably. Unlike intentions alone, these mechanisms guarantee that the desired outcomes are achieved consistently, fostering trust and maintaining a positive reputation. Here's an example that ties in with the section above. You can think of Automated Code Reviews as a mechanism where hoping developers remember to follow your checklist is a good intention.

As a business leader or engineering manager, you play a crucial role in the implementation of mechanisms. Your decisions on consistency and adaptability are key. Don't fall into the trap that many do and assume that just because a process or mechanism is in place, you have to follow it. If you know a better way, you have the authority to speak up and make improvements. This empowerment is crucial in driving operational excellence and process improvement.

Consistency in Action: Operating consistently is a hallmark of effective mechanisms despite fluctuating circumstances. This consistency stabilizes, ensuring the organization's actions align consistently with its goals. New managers should exercise caution when developing mechanisms, as they should only commit to those they can see through. To identify and develop effective mechanisms, it's crucial to understand your team or organization's specific needs and challenges. This understanding is not just about ticking boxes, it's about appreciating the unique circumstances and requirements of your team, making them feel heard and valued. This can be done through regular communication and feedback and by studying best practices in your industry.

Adaptability and Flexibility: Effective mechanisms need to be adaptable and flexible, allowing organizations to navigate changes while continuing to pursue operational excellence. In this context, 'adaptability' refers to the ability of a mechanism to adjust to changes in its environment or objectives. This adaptability supports ongoing success in dynamic environments. For example, a mechanism could be a project management tool that allows for easy reassignment of tasks when team members are unavailable due to unforeseen circumstances.

Some of the benefits of implementing mechanisms in your team include:

Efficiency and Optimization: Mechanisms streamline processes, eliminate inefficiencies, and optimize resources. They act as the engine driving the organization toward greater efficiency, utilizing tools such as automated workflows, performance metrics, and feedback loops.

Simplicity: When designing mechanisms, it is important to remember that they should only be as complex as is needed to solve the problem at hand. Adding unnecessary complexity to a mechanism can increase costs, maintenance issues, and potential failure points. Therefore, it is essential to carefully evaluate the problem and its requirements before designing the mechanism, ensuring that it is both practical and efficient while keeping complexity to a minimum. Sometimes, you only need a checklist and a tool to complete them.

Risk Mitigation: Mechanisms are not just tools but your security blanket in mitigating risks by establishing standardized processes and protocols. This isn't just about minimizing the likelihood of errors or deviations hindering operational excellence, it's about instilling a sense of security and confidence in your operations. Automating mechanisms can significantly mitigate risks caused by manual touches to application code. By automating standardized processes and protocols, organizations can reduce the likelihood of errors or deviations and ensure operational excellence. This helps manage risks effectively and contributes to sustained high performance, reinforcing your confidence in the system.

To sum up, while good intentions provide vision and motivation, achieving lasting change requires the support of reliable mechanisms. In this context, 'good intentions' refer to the desire or aspiration to achieve a certain outcome. At the same time, 'mechanisms' are the practical means through which organizations translate these intentions into consistent, reliable, and efficient actions. Mechanisms are not a replacement for good intentions but rather a necessary tool to realize these intentions, forming the foundation for success in a dynamic business landscape. In other words, good intentions set the direction, and mechanisms provide the roadmap to get there.

Let's look at an example:

Toyota has always focused on continuous improvement and operational excellence. In manufacturing, they use the "andon cord" mechanism to ensure that every production process is consistent and reliable. Another example is Amazon, which uses a sophisticated inventory management system to ensure timely order delivery.

The andon cord is a simple but effective mechanism that enables any worker on the production line to stop the entire production process if they notice a problem. The cord is located above each worker's workstation, and pulling it alerts the supervisor and the rest of the team that an issue needs to be addressed.

When a worker pulls the andon cord, the entire production line stops, allowing everyone to identify and fix the problem before it can cause further issues. This mechanism ensures that every part of the manufacturing process is subject to continuous improvement, making it more efficient, reliable, and consistent.

Over time, Toyota has refined this mechanism, integrating it with other tools and processes to create a culture of continuous improvement throughout the organization. In this context, 'continuous improvement' refers to the ongoing effort to improve products, services, or processes. The andon cord has become a symbol of Toyota's commitment to quality, efficiency, and reliability, and it continues to be an essential part of its manufacturing process today.

In summary, the andon cord is an example of a mechanism that Toyota uses to ensure that every step of the production process is consistent and reliable. This mechanism allows workers to stop the production line if there is a problem, ensuring that issues are identified and fixed before they can cause any further problems. The andon cord is an essential part of Toyota's culture of continuous improvement, which has helped it become one of the world's most successful and respected companies.

Having good intentions, such as building a quality car, is a great starting point, but achieving consistent and reliable results is challenging without your role in implementing reliable mechanisms. Toyota's focus on building a quality car is supported by implementing mechanisms such as the andon cord, which ensures that every step of the production process is consistent and reliable.

In contrast, a company that only focuses on good intentions and lacks reliable mechanisms may face significant challenges. For instance, a car manufacturer that only focuses on building a quality car without implementing reliable mechanisms may struggle to identify and fix issues on the production line. This could lead to vehicles that do not meet the desired quality standards, resulting in customer dissatisfaction and negatively impacting the company's reputation. This example underscores the importance of mechanisms in translating good intentions into consistent and reliable actions. It also highlights the potential risks of not implementing mechanisms, such as quality issues and customer dissatisfaction, which can have serious implications for the business.

Therefore, having good intentions is a great starting point. Still, it is essential to have reliable mechanisms to translate these intentions into consistent and reliable actions. Toyota's focus on mechanisms such as the andon cord has enabled it to achieve consistent results in building quality cars, contributing to its success and positive reputation in the automotive industry. As an engineering manager or business leader, you can implement similar mechanisms in your organization, driving it towards operational excellence and sustained high performance.ng manager or business leader, you have the power to implement similar mechanisms in your organization, driving it towards operational excellence and sustained high performance.

Good intentions cannot drive success in today's fast-paced and competitive business environment. Organizations that rely solely on good intentions without a clear plan or set of mechanisms often struggle to achieve their goals and objectives. While good intentions are important, they are insufficient to ensure everyone works efficiently and effectively towards the same objectives.

On the other hand, mechanisms are the tools and processes that teams use to drive their work forward and achieve their goals. They provide a clear structure for decision-making and action, ensuring everyone is on the same page and working towards the same objective.

For example, if a team is working on a project, having a set of mechanisms in place can help them achieve their objectives more efficiently. This could include regular meetings to discuss progress, clear communication channels to ensure everyone is informed, and performance metrics to track progress and make adjustments as needed. A common misconception is that mechanisms are very complex and take months or years to develop when, in reality, it's a defined process backed by the consistency to keep at it. One of the simplest mechanisms I've created is a simple reminder and filter that shows all incoming tickets between team syncs (24 hours on weekdays and up to 72 on weekends) so that the team can review, reassign, and prioritize customer requests daily. This is important because not all stakeholders view different issues at the same level, and important customer issues may be lost if they are not prioritized correctly.

By emphasizing mechanisms over good intentions, teams can create a culture of excellence based on efficiency, productivity, and results. This helps teams achieve their goals and fosters a sense of accountability and ownership among team members, leading to increased engagement and motivation.

Observability

Understanding how software systems behave in production becomes increasingly crucial as they become complex. This is where observability comes into play. With observability, we gain insights into the internal workings of our systems, making it easier to troubleshoot issues and optimize performance. In this chapter, we'll explore the concept of observability and its importance in modern software development. We'll also dive into fundamental techniques and tools for building observable systems, including logging, metrics, and tracing. So, join me as we explore the fascinating world of observability and learn how to build systems that are easier to understand, troubleshoot, and maintain.

Principles of Observability

Observability is a vital aspect of any software system. It refers to gaining insights into the system's inner workings by analyzing data generated by its components. The three primary pillars of observability are logs, metrics, and tracing.

Logs are records of events that occur within a system. They provide a chronological record of what happened, when, and who or what initiated the event. Logs can be used for troubleshooting, debugging, and auditing.

Metrics are numerical values that measure the performance of a system. They can track resource usage, identify bottlenecks, and detect anomalies. Metrics can be collected over time to create time-series data, which can be used for capacity planning and trend analysis.

Tracing involves tracking the flow of requests through a system. It provides a detailed view of how individual requests are processed and can help identify performance issues that might not be apparent from metrics alone. Tracing can be used to visualize the dependencies between components and to understand the impact of changes to the system.

Key Metrics for Tier1 Backend Application Services

As a backend service for a web application, it is essential to monitor several key metrics to ensure smooth operations. Some of the metrics that should be monitored include:

Latency: "I wanna go fast!"

Latency is a crucial metric to monitor when ensuring a service's optimal performance. It is the delay between a request being made and the response being received. High latency can cause bottlenecks, leading to poor user experience and decreased productivity.

Several factors can cause high latency and bottlenecks. One of the most common reasons is network congestion. If the network is congested, data transmission can slow down, leading to increased latency. Another cause can be inadequate server resources. If the server is overloaded or doesn't have enough resources, it can slow down the processing of requests and increase latency.

To resolve these issues, monitoring latency and promptly identifying bottlenecks is essential. One way to do this is by using performance monitoring tools. These tools can help identify the root cause of the issue, such as network congestion or server overload. Once the issue is identified, appropriate measures can be taken to resolve it.

For example, if congestion is the issue, the network can be optimized to reduce it. This can be done by increasing bandwidth, reducing the number of users on the network, or using a more efficient network protocol. If the issue is inadequate server resources, the server can be upgraded or optimized to handle more requests efficiently.

Latency can have a significant impact on the customer

experience. Slow response times can lead to frustration and dissatisfaction, causing customers to abandon the service or website altogether. For example, in the case of online shopping, a slow checkout process can discourage customers from completing their purchases or lead them to switch to a competitor's website. In addition, latency can impact real-time applications such as gaming or video conferencing, causing delays that affect the user's ability to communicate or interact with others. Therefore, monitoring and managing latency is crucial to ensuring customers have a positive experience and stay engaged with the service.

When looking at latency metrics, it's important to understand the difference between P95 and P90. P95 refers to the 95th percentile of response times, while P90 refers to the 90th percentile. The higher the percentile, the longer the response time.

While P95 and P90 are valuable measures of typical response times, it is also essential to look for outliers. Outliers are response times that are significantly longer than the rest. These outliers can indicate issues with the system that need to be addressed.

For example, if the P95 response time is 1 second, but there are occasional response times of 10 seconds, it's important to investigate those outliers. Issues like network latency, database contention, or other performance bottlenecks could cause them.

By identifying and addressing outliers, teams can improve their systems' overall performance and reliability. So, when analyzing latency metrics, it's important to look beyond just P95 and P90 and identify any outliers affecting performance.

Tracing is a crucial tool for identifying and resolving latency issues in an application. With tracing, you can track the performance of each application component and identify the ones causing delays and contributing the most to latency. For example, by tracing a call, you can identify which part of the call is experiencing the longest delay, allowing you to look at the parts of the application that contribute the most to latency issues.

Tracing works by creating a log of each step of a request as it moves through the application. This log includes information about each step's duration, allowing you to identify the components causing delays. You can also use tracing to identify patterns in your application's performance, such as requests that consistently take longer than others or components that frequently cause delays.

Once you've identified the components contributing the most to latency, you can focus your efforts on optimizing them. This might involve reducing the number of requests to that component, optimizing the code, or adding more resources to handle the load.

In summary, monitoring latency is crucial for ensuring optimal performance in your application or service. Tracing can pinpoint and optimize the components causing delays to improve overall performance. High latency can cause bottlenecks and lead to poor user experience, so it's essential to identify the root cause of the issue and take appropriate measures to reduce it.

Considerations when Implementing Observability

Integrating observability into the development process is a crucial concept that ensures that the entire development lifecycle is monitored and optimized for peak performance. Observability refers to gaining insight into the complex systems and applications of the modern IT landscape.

By integrating observability into the development process, developers can ensure they build reliable, scalable, and maintainable systems from the start. This includes monitoring the application's performance and identifying any issues or bottlenecks early in the development cycle.

One key benefit of integrating observability into the development process is identifying and addressing issues before they become critical problems. This helps reduce downtime and prevent costly outages from impacting the business's bottom line. Additionally, it ensures that the application performs optimally throughout its lifecycle, which can increase user satisfaction and loyalty.

To achieve observability, developers need to implement various tools and techniques that enable them to monitor and analyze the application's performance. This includes logging, metrics, and tracing, among other things. By using these tools, developers can gain a deep understanding of how the application is performing and identify any issues that need to be addressed.

Logging

Logging, the process of recording information about software execution, is fundamental to understanding system behavior, diagnosing issues, and ensuring operational stability. It is critical in observability, one of the three pillars alongside metrics and traces. Logging provides detailed insights into an application's inner workings, enabling developers to comprehensively observe and understand system state and behavior.

Logs can be categorized into various types, each serving a specific purpose. Event logs capture specific events, such as user actions and important milestones in the application's workflow. Error logs record errors, exceptions, and failures, offering insights into the nature and cause of problems. Audit logs track access and changes to data and resources, often essential for security and compliance. Transaction logs detail business processes and data integrity, while system logs provide information about the underlying infrastructure, including operating system and hardware-related logs.

Effective logging requires using different log levels to indicate the severity and nature of log entries. DEBUG logs provide detailed information useful for diagnosing problems, whereas INFO logs record general operational entries. WARN logs indicate potential issues that are not necessarily errors, while ERROR logs capture error events that might still allow the application to continue running. FATAL logs denote severe errors that lead to application termination.

Implementing best practices in logging is crucial for maximizing its benefits. Consistency in log format and structure facilitates parsing and analysis. Including contextual information such as timestamps, user IDs, session IDs, and transaction IDs enhances the utility of logs. Performance considerations are vital; logging should not significantly impact application performance, and asynchronous logging can help mitigate this. Security and privacy concerns must be addressed by avoiding logging sensitive information and using techniques like masking or redaction where necessary. Additionally, log rotation and retention policies are important for managing log file size and complying with regulatory requirements.

Several logging frameworks and tools are available to streamline the logging process. Popular logging frameworks include Log4j, SLF4J, and Logback for Java, NLog and Serilog for .NET, and Python's logging module. Centralized logging aggregates logs from different sources into a centralized system and is essential for efficient log management. Tools like the ELK Stack (Elasticsearch, Logstash, Kibana), Splunk, and Graylog facilitate log aggregation, searching, and visualization. Log analysis tools enhance monitoring by applying pattern matching, statistical analysis, and machine learning to detect anomalies and gain insights.

Designing an effective logging strategy involves defining log levels, identifying key events to log, and determining appropriate log storage and management solutions. Integrating logging with CI/CD pipelines ensures that it is part of the continuous integration and deployment processes, allowing for automated log validation and early issue detection. Handling log data at scale presents challenges that can be addressed with distributed logging systems, log compression, and scalable storage solutions.

Real-world case studies illustrate how companies use logging to improve system reliability, security, and performance. These examples highlight the critical role of logging in, diagnosing, and resolving issues, as demonstrated through post-mortem analyses of incidents. In the future, machine learning and AI will play an increasingly significant role in log analysis, automatically detecting anomalies and predicting issues. Observability platforms are integrating logging with metrics and traces to provide a comprehensive view of system health, and efforts are underway to standardize log formats and improve interoperability between tools.

Several logging frameworks and tools are available to help developers implement observability in their applications. Here are some commonly used ones (which is in no way a holistic list, and I do not discuss any particular benefits of choosing one over the other):

Log4j: Log4j is a popular logging framework for Java applications. It provides a flexible and configurable logging architecture that can be used to log messages at different levels (e.g., debug, info, error). Log4j can write logs to various destinations, such as a file, console, or database.

Logback: Logback is a successor to Log4j and provides a similar logging architecture. It is designed to be faster and more efficient than Log4j and offers additional features, such as automatic configuration file reloading.

Fluentd: Fluentd is a logging tool that collects, filters, and routes logs from various sources to different destinations. It supports various log formats and protocols and can aggregate logs from multiple servers.

ELK Stack: The ELK Stack (Elasticsearch, Logstash, and Kibana) is a popular logging and monitoring solution for collecting, storing, and analyzing log data. Elasticsearch stores the log data, Logstash collects and filters it, and Kibana visualizes and analyzes it.

Graylog: Graylog is another logging and monitoring solution for collecting, storing, and analyzing log data. It provides a web interface for searching and analyzing log data and can generate alerts based on specific patterns.

Tracing

Tracing, in the context of distributed systems, is crucial to modern software engineering. It involves tracking the flow of requests through various system components, enabling developers to understand and diagnose performance issues, identify bottlenecks, and ensure system reliability. Effective tracing allows teams to visualize how data moves through their applications, facilitating quicker problem identification and more efficient troubleshooting.

Regarding tracing tools, X-Ray and Datadog are two popular options developers can use to trace requests as they travel through distributed systems. For instance, AWS X-Ray, provided by Amazon Web Services (AWS), can trace requests as they travel through distributed systems, such as a microservices architecture. It visualizes the trace data and can be used to identify bottlenecks and performance issues, like a slow database query. X-Ray supports tracing for AWS services and other popular frameworks such as Node.js, Java, and .NET Core.

Datadog, on the other hand, is a monitoring and analytics platform that provides tracing capabilities for distributed systems. It allows developers to trace requests across multiple services and visualizes the trace data. Datadog supports tracing for several popular frameworks, such as Node.js, Java, Python, Ruby, and .NET.

When comparing X-Ray and Datadog tracing capabilities, there are some key differences. X-Ray is tightly integrated with AWS services, making it a good option for developers using AWS services. It seamlessly integrates AWS Lambda, EC2, ECS, and other services. On the other hand, Datadog provides integration with AWS services but may require additional configuration, such as setting up IAM roles and permissions. X-Ray is relatively easy to set up and use, especially for AWS services. Developers can enable X-Ray tracing for their applications with just a few lines of code. Datadog, however, may require more configuration and setup.

Both X-Ray and Datadog visualize the trace data. However, Datadog, with its extensive customization options, empowers developers to tailor the visualization of the trace data to their specific needs. It also offers features such as anomaly detection and alerting based on trace data. Regarding pricing, X-Ray is included in the AWS Free Tier and has a pay-as-you-go pricing model for usage beyond the free tier. Datadog has a subscription-based pricing model.

In summary, both X-Ray and Datadog provide tracing capabilities for distributed systems. Due to its tight integration with AWS services, X-Ray is a good option for developers using AWS services. At the same time, Datadog provides more flexibility regarding visualization capabilities and additional features such as anomaly detection and alerting. Developers must consider their specific needs and use cases when choosing between X-Ray and Datadog to ensure they make the most informed decision.

Dashboards and Alerting

Clear dashboards and properly set up alerts are critical for observability in modern software applications. Dashboards provide an at-a-glance view of application performance. Clear dashboards visually represent the application's performance, allowing developers to identify any issues or bottlenecks affecting it quickly. Dashboards should display key metrics such as response time, error rate, throughput, and any custom metrics relevant to the application.

Alerts help identify and respond to critical issues. Alerts notify developers when an application performance or behavior issue occurs. Properly set up alerts can help developers respond quickly to critical issues, reducing downtime and minimizing the impact on the business. Alerts should be configured based on specific thresholds or patterns in the data, such as when response time exceeds a certain threshold or error rates increase above a certain level.

Clear dashboards and alerts are not just tools but accelerators for issue identification. Properly setting up alerts can help developers quickly identify the root cause when an issue arises, speeding up the troubleshooting process. Dashboards can be used to drill down into specific areas of the application to identify where the issue is occurring, while alerts can provide contextual information to help developers understand the nature and severity of the issue, making the process more efficient and productive.

Clear dashboards and properly set up alerts are not just for individual use but for team collaboration. They can improve communication and collaboration between different teams involved in the application's development and operation. By providing a shared view of the application's performance and issues, teams can work together to identify and resolve issues more effectively, fostering a sense of unity and shared responsibility.

In summary, clear dashboards and properly set up alerts are critical for observability in modern software applications. They visually represent the application's performance, help identify and respond to critical issues, aid in troubleshooting, and improve team collaboration. Developers should ensure that their dashboards and alerts are properly configured and maintained to ensure the application performs optimally and meets the business's needs.

Weekly Operations Meetings

A weekly ops meeting is an effective mechanism to constantly review dashboards and identify and address any issues or bottlenecks. Here's why:

Reiterating the role of the weekly ops meeting in promoting continuous improvement empowers teams to review the application's performance and identify areas for enhancement. This instills a sense of responsibility and motivation in each team member to devise a plan to address any issues or bottlenecks, making them feel motivated and committed to the process.

Increases visibility: A weekly ops meeting increases visibility into the application's performance by providing a shared view of the dashboards and metrics. The meeting allows different teams involved in the application's development and operation to understand its performance better and identify any issues or bottlenecks.

The weekly ops meeting is a collaborative platform that brings together different teams involved in the application's development and operation. It encourages the sharing of perspectives and insights, fostering a spirit of teamwork. Together, these teams can identify and address any issues or bottlenecks, promoting a more efficient and effective operation.

Helps prioritize work: A weekly operations meeting can help prioritize work by identifying which issues or bottlenecks are most critical and must be addressed first. The meeting can also discuss the severity and impact of different issues and devise a plan to address them based on their priority.

In addition to reviewing dashboards and metrics, it's important to include on-call handoff notes in the weekly ops meeting agenda. This helps ensure a smooth transition of responsibilities between on-call engineers, which is crucial for maintaining system availability and uptime.

Assigning action items to engineers is crucial to the weekly ops meeting. It ensures that any issues or bottlenecks identified during the meeting are effectively addressed and resolved. By assigning specific tasks to individual engineers, the meeting promotes accountability and ensures progress toward resolving issues, thereby enhancing the overall efficiency of the operation.

Underlining the customer-centric approach, the weekly operations meeting should be used to discuss any customer-impacting code fixes that need to be made. This ensures that the team is aware of any issues affecting customers and can work together to develop a plan to address them as quickly as possible, making the audience feel the importance of their role in customer satisfaction.

A weekly ops meeting is an effective mechanism for constantly reviewing dashboards and ensuring any issues or bottlenecks are identified and addressed. The meeting promotes continuous improvement, increases visibility, facilitates collaboration, and helps prioritize work. Developers should ensure that the meeting has a clear agenda and defined goals to make the most of it.

Using Observability for Incident Response

Incident response refers to detecting, investigating, and resolving unexpected events that can negatively impact systems, applications, or services. These unexpected events could be system downtime, server crashes, application errors, security breaches, or any other system anomalies affecting an IT environment's performance or security.

Observability, on the other hand, is the ability to measure and monitor the state and behavior of a system or application in real-time. It involves collecting and analyzing data from various sources to gain insights into how a system performs and can be improved.

Now, why is observability important for incident detection and response? Well, incidents can happen anytime, and it's essential to have a system that can detect and respond to them quickly to minimize their impact. Observability allows you to gain real-time insights into your system, making it easier to detect issues as soon as they arise.

With observability, you can collect data from various sources, including logs, metrics, and traces, and use this information to detect abnormal behavior or performance issues. Additionally, observability allows you to investigate issues by drilling down into specific components, such as servers or applications, to understand the root cause of an incident.

Overall, observability helps you to build a proactive approach to incident response, enabling you to detect and resolve issues before they escalate into major problems. This capability is particularly important in complex IT environments, where issues can be hard to detect and troubleshoot, and the cost of downtime can be significant. Incident response refers to detecting, investigating, and resolving unexpected events that can negatively impact systems, applications, or services. These unexpected events could be anything from system downtime, server crashes, application errors, security breaches, or any other system anomalies that could affect the performance or security of an IT environment.

Observability and Continuous Improvement

Observability data can proactively identify bottlenecks and issues in distributed systems. Tracing the root cause of an issue can be challenging in such complex systems. However, by incorporating observability into the continuous improvement process, teams can better understand how different system components interact with each other and how they impact overall performance.

One essential tool for observability is tracing. Tracing can identify connection issues to third-party APIs, databases, and other external services. By tracing the flow of requests and responses between different components, teams can better understand how these components interact and where the bottlenecks occur. This information can then be used to improve and optimize the system's performance.

Using observability data to identify bottlenecks proactively can help teams improve their systems' reliability and performance. By incorporating observability into the continuous improvement process and tracing issues in third-party connections, teams can significantly improve tier-1 services. You should discuss all long-running calls during your weekly operations meeting.

Observability and Organizational Culture

There are several reasons why teams may resist adopting observability practices. One main reason is that it can be seen as an additional burden that takes time and resources away from other projects. Some team members may also resist change, particularly if they have used the same tools and methods for a long time. Additionally, there may be concerns about data privacy and security, particularly if the observability tools collect sensitive information.

Another reason for resistance may be a lack of understanding of observability and how it can benefit the team. Some team members may not see the value in collecting and analyzing data or understand how it can be used to identify trends and improve services. They may also be concerned about the tools' complexity and the amount of training required to use them effectively.

Finally, there may be organizational or cultural barriers to adoption. For example, some organizations may not have a culture of continuous improvement or may not prioritize investment in new tools and technologies. In these cases, it may be necessary to build a business case for adopting observability practices and to work to change the culture around data-driven decision-making.

Addressing each barrier mentioned earlier is important to overcome resistance to adopting observability practices. Here are some strategies that can be used to overcome each of these obstacles:

Address the time and resource burden: One way to address this concern is to show the team how observability can save time and resources in the long run by identifying and addressing issues before they become major problems. It may also be helpful to prioritize observability as a key aspect of the team's work and to allocate resources specifically for observability-related tasks.

Address resistance to change: To overcome resistance to change, it's important to involve team members in the decision-making process and get their input on which observability tools and practices best suit their needs. Training and support to help team members transition to new tools and methods may also be helpful.

Address concerns around data privacy and security: To address these concerns, it's important to ensure that observability tools are designed with security and privacy in mind. This may involve implementing data encryption, access controls, and other security measures. It may also be helpful to train team members to handle sensitive data.

Address a lack of understanding: To overcome a lack of understanding about observability, it's important to provide clear and concise explanations of what observability is and how it can benefit the team. Training on using observability tools effectively and examples of how observability has led to improvements in other organizations may also be helpful.

Address organizational and cultural barriers: To overcome them, building a business case for adopting observability practices and demonstrating the value of data-driven decision-making is important. Working with leadership to create a culture of continuous improvement and prioritize investment in new tools and technologies may also be helpful.

Managers need to ensure that they can effectively convey how observability can help the team achieve its goals when communicating the value of observability to team members. This can be a challenge, particularly if team members are resistant to change or skeptical about the value of observability.

To overcome this challenge, managers can provide concrete examples of how observability has significantly improved tier-1 services. This can help team members see the tangible benefits of observability and understand how it can help them be more effective in their roles.

In addition to providing examples, managers should also be clear about how observability data will be used to identify trends and areas for improvement and how it will be incorporated into the continuous improvement process. By providing this level of detail, managers can help team members understand how observability fits into the broader context of the team's work.

Finally, managers need to be patient and understanding when communicating the value of observability to team members. It's natural for people to be resistant to change, particularly if they are comfortable with existing processes and tools. By listening to team members' concerns and addressing them thoughtfully and respectfully, managers can help build buy-in and ensure that the team can fully leverage the benefits of observability. When communicating the value of observability to team members, managers must ensure that they can effectively convey how it can help the team achieve its goals. This can be a challenge, particularly if team members resist change or are skeptical about the value of observability.

Case Studies

One real-world example of observability preventing something terrible from happening occurred in 2019 when a major airline company experienced a critical issue that could have resulted in a catastrophic outcome. The airline's system, which managed flight scheduling, went down, and the company could not see which planes were available, where they were, and whether they were fit to fly.

Fortunately, the company had implemented an observability system that tracked all the system's components, including the application, infrastructure, and network. The system quickly alerted the IT team about the problem and provided them with the necessary information to diagnose and fix it.

The IT team discovered that the issue was caused by an outdated software component that had failed to update properly. They fixed the problem before it caused any major disruptions or safety issues. Had the observability system not been in place, the airline could have experienced significant delays, flight cancellations, and even accidents.

This incident highlights the importance of observability in preventing catastrophic outcomes. With an observability system, companies can quickly detect and respond to issues, ensuring critical systems remain up and running. It also helps to maintain customer satisfaction, as disruptions are minimized and issues are resolved before they affect the customer experience.

Data-Driven Decision Making

Data is crucial in software engineering, guiding decisions and driving improvements. By analyzing data, teams can gain valuable insights that help them make informed decisions, improve processes, and achieve operational excellence. This section explores the importance of data-driven decision-making and how metrics and insights can help teams achieve their goals.

The Power of Informed Choices

Data-driven decision-making empowers software engineering teams to navigate complex challenges and opportunities rapidly. By embracing data as a guiding force, teams move beyond intuition and gut feelings to make choices founded on empirical evidence.

Data-driven decisions are rooted in objective information, minimizing biases and assumptions. However, it is essential to recognize that statistics can still be subject to certain biases. For example, selection bias can occur when the data used for analysis does not represent the studied population. Similarly, confirmation bias can occur when individuals seek out or interpret data to confirm their beliefs or opinions.

To mitigate these biases, it's important to approach data critically and consider multiple sources and perspectives. It's also important to be transparent about any limitations or potential biases in the data used so that others can make informed decisions based on the available information.

Finally, data-driven insights allow teams to identify issues before they escalate, enabling proactive solutions.

Metrics

Metrics are the barometers that gauge the health and progress of software engineering endeavors. Just as a barometer indicates changing weather conditions, metrics indicate shifts in project health, code quality, and team performance. Teams with relevant metrics can assess their performance, detect anomalies, and adjust their course. Choosing the right metrics is crucial for effective monitoring of software engineering projects. Incorrect metrics can lead to inaccurate assessments and misguided decisions, ultimately impacting the project's success. Therefore, it's important to carefully evaluate the metrics used and ensure they align with the project goals and objectives. By selecting the appropriate metrics, teams can gain valuable insights into project progress and make informed decisions to help them achieve their desired outcomes.

Performance Tracking: Metrics provide a clear view of team and project performance, offering insights into bottlenecks and inefficiencies.

Early Warnings: Metrics play a crucial role in tracking the performance of a project or business. However, sometimes, there may be certain irregularities or anomalies in these metrics, which can act as early warnings for potential problems. These anomalies can alert the teams to address the underlying issues before they escalate into more significant problems. By paying attention to these early warning signals, teams can take proactive measures to mitigate the risks and prevent any negative impact on the overall performance of the project or business. Thus, anomalies in metrics are important indicators that should not be ignored and addressed promptly to ensure the success and sustainability of the project or business.

Insights from Data: Unveiling Opportunities

Data insight is valuable information that can be extracted from data analysis. It is a discovery or realization derived from data, which can help a business understand its operations better and make informed decisions. Data insights can reveal hidden patterns, trends, and relationships, which can be used to optimize business processes, improve the customer experience, and identify new growth opportunities. Data insights result from analyzing and interpreting data using various analytical tools and techniques, such as data mining, machine learning, statistical analysis, and predictive modeling. Data insights are actionable information that can help businesses gain a competitive advantage and make informed decisions.

A real-world example of data insights in software engineering could be analyzing software usage data to identify areas of the product that customers use frequently or do not use. This insight can help the development team prioritize their efforts and work on more important customer features. Additionally, the team can use data insights to identify and fix bugs causing the most user issues. The team can identify common complaints or feature requests by analyzing customer feedback data and use this information to improve the product. In this example, data insights help the software development team optimize their development efforts, fix bugs, and improve customer satisfaction.

Enabling Continuous Process Improvement

In the realm of operational excellence, process improvement is a continuous journey. Data-driven decision-making provides the roadmap, allowing teams to identify which paths lead to the most significant gains. Like a skilled driver adjusting their route based on real-time traffic updates, teams adapt their processes based on data insights to navigate toward optimal efficiency and quality.

Real-Time Adjustments: Data-driven decisions allow for swift adjustments as conditions change, ensuring optimal progress.

Iterative Refinement: By embracing data, teams ensure that their process improvement efforts are well-informed and iterative.

Aligning with Operational Excellence

Operational excellence requires constant monitoring,

evaluation, and refinement—an endeavor well-suited for data-driven methodologies. Just as a ship's captain relies on navigational instruments, teams rely on data to navigate the waters of software engineering, ensuring that their actions align with their pursuit of excellence.

Precision in Execution: Data-driven insights guide teams to execute their tasks precisely, minimizing wastage.

Aligned Actions: Data-driven decisions ensure that actions are aligned with the overarching goals of operational excellence.

Conclusion

In software engineering, data-based decisions are essential to achieving optimal performance. Data metrics and insights help teams improve efficiency and quality. However, it's important to remember that sometimes anecdotes can provide valuable information that conflicts with data. In these situations, it's crucial to prioritize the anecdote over the data.

Data is invaluable in pursuing operational excellence. It provides a compass for decision-making, enabling teams to make informed choices, identify patterns, and uncover areas for improvement. By embracing evidence-based decisions, teams transform their actions from mere conjectures into calculated steps toward software engineering excellence.

The human touch is essential in our journey. Personal anecdotes and qualitative insights provide a nuanced perspective that complements the data's quantitative nature. When anecdotes and data present inconsistencies, it's wise to prioritize the anecdote. Human intuition and contextual understanding can reveal aspects that data alone may overlook.

Jeff Bezos, the visionary founder of Amazon, emphasized the importance of this interplay between data and anecdotes. In one of his talks, he noted, "We can have data without information, but we cannot have information without data." This encapsulates the essence of using data to extract meaningful information, yet it doesn't discount the power of anecdotes in providing context and depth to decision-making."

Bezos further highlighted the significance of anecdotes, stating, "If you have a good anecdote, the data can become your enemy." This underscores the idea that anecdotes, backed by credibility and relevance, can challenge or provide a nuanced perspective on the quantitative data.

This philosophy implies that while metrics and data-driven insights are crucial in software engineering, they should complement anecdotes' rich context and understanding. Teams should be open to the idea that sometimes, the most meaningful insights come from the stories of those on the ground, navigating the challenges and triumphs of the software development process.

Two critical factors are essential to achieving operational excellence in software engineering - data and anecdotes. Data provides objective insights to guide teams, while anecdotes offer context and depth to decision-making. Jeff Bezos wisely reminds us that when anecdotes and data disagree, giving weight to the anecdote is a strategic choice. It acknowledges the intrinsic value of human experience in navigating the unpredictable seas of software development.

ABOUT THE AUTHOR

Joshua McDonald, a dynamic engineering leader and problem solver, brings over fifteen years of experience in software engineering. His academic credentials include a Master of Business Administration and a Master of Science in Analytics from Georgia Tech, alongside a Computer Science degree. Joshua's expertise spans the computer, network security, and healthcare industries, where he has led diverse teams of engineering, data science, and cybersecurity professionals. Notably, his career has taken him across Europe and the United States, showcasing his adaptability and global perspective.

Joshua McDonald, known for valuing people over processes and continuous learning, has held significant roles at Amazon, Fanatics, Inc., and AWS, among others. His skill set includes proficiency in Go (Golang), SQL databases, JavaScript, and public speaking. Joshua's leadership is a standout, marked by his ability to inspire teams, set clear directions, and foster a positive, growth-oriented environment. These qualities have consistently led to high team performance and successful project outcomes.

Joshua's extensive international experience includes working in both Europe and the United States, showcasing his adaptability and global perspective. His career highlights include successfully leading major technical migrations, enhancing operational excellence, and driving the public launch of key platforms.

With a history of solving complex problems and a deep-rooted passion for mentoring, Joshua McDonald is unwaveringly dedicated to advancing the field of engineering management through innovative solutions and a relentless pursuit of continuous improvement.

www.ingramcontent.com/pod-product-compliance
Lightning Source LLC
Chambersburg PA
CBHW052257220526
45471CB00001B/380